Trowel & Error

Over 700 Shortcuts,  Tips & Remedies for the Gardener

Sharon Lovejoy

WORKMAN PUBLISHING • NEW YORK

Library of Congress Cataloging-in-Publication Data

Lovejoy, Sharon, 1945–
    Trowel & error : over 700 tips, remedies & shortcuts for the
    gardener / by Sharon Lovejoy.
        p. cm.
    Includes bibliographical references (p.).
    ISBN 0-7611-2632-5 (alk. paper)
        1. Gardening—Miscellanea. I. Title: Trowel and error.
    II. Title.

SB453.L9334 2003
635—dc21   2002028880

Book design by Janet Parker

Workman Publishing Company, Inc.
708 Broadway
New York, NY 10003-9555
www.workman.com

Printed in Singapore

First printing: February 2003
10 9 8 7 6 5 4 3 2 1

Dedicated to my heroes—
John Rhinus Clarke, John Richard Arnold,
Frank Gander, John Muir,
Noah Wm Arnold, Albert Blifeld,
and my incredible husband,
Jeff Prostovich.

ACKNOWLEDGMENTS

THIS BOOK WOULD NOT HAVE HAPPENED WITHOUT THE WORK of my brilliant editor Ruth Sullivan. Ruth has a magical touch and a fine sensibility, and when working with me knew how to blend just the right amount of toughness and honesty with encouragement and humor. She turned my gigantic mound of word-compost into a rich, reader-friendly humus, and in the workings she turned me into a better writer, and herself into an even better gardener.

Heartfelt thanks to Peter Workman for believing in me and for continuing the tradition of publishing with integrity and professionalism. Special thanks to Lisa Hollander of the art department, and designer Janet Parker, who absorbed my manuscript and skillfully and intuitively created a playful and life-filled book. Thanks also to Elizabeth Gaynor for producing the book, and Anne Cherry, the project manager.

Thanks to the helpful staff at the Santa Barbara Botanic Gardens and Santa Barbara Museum of Natural History, entomologists and zoologists at the Los Angeles County Museum of Natural History, entomologists and invertebrate zoologists at the American Museum of Natural History in New York, Bill Quarles, Bio-Integral Resource Center, The Humane Society of the United States, Nancy Hillenburg, Pat Reppert, Betsy Williams, Eleanor Jantzen, Marion Owen, Master

Gardener and teacher, Sharon Christian Aderman (who contributed mightily to my Maine library), my assistant Danielle Shea, Claude Maher, Sherry Hyman, Patricia Fly, Patricia Cowan, Lucy Harrell, Laurie Otto, Ethyl Pochocki, Ed Sampson of Mourning Cloak Botanic Garden, taught to him by his mother Jessie Sampson. Carlos Quijano, Coast of Maine Organics, Ralph Bronner, Andy Lopez, Invisible Gardeners, Mary Muncy, Agatha Youngblood, Renee Shepherd of Renee's Garden, staff at Rodale Gardens in Emmaus, Pennsylvania, Phil Torchio, PhD., the Pueblo of Acoma, Research Staff of the Smithsonian, Gertrude Foster, Mary Porter, Cambria Writers Workshop, Jack and Olga Essex, John and Augustine Clarke, Abigail Lovejoy, Lynn Karlin, Marta Morse, Laurie Lovejoy Prather, Patricia and Ruby Berry, Kate Stearns, Diane DeWeir, Marilyn Brewer, Peggy Phillips and Francesca Bolognini (for tending my gardens and birds when I'm away), and the hundreds of readers who sent me suggestions and hints (wish I had kept all your notes and e-mails).

Finally, no words can convey my gratitude to my husband, Jeffrey Prostovich. He was with me every step of the way, from brewing stinking potions in our kitchen, testing recipes, and blotting aphids, to ferreting out resources, organizations, and scientific information. He is my best critic and the partner of a lifetime.

Sharon Lovejoy

Contents

Part I: Outdoor Gardening

Part II: Indoor Gardening

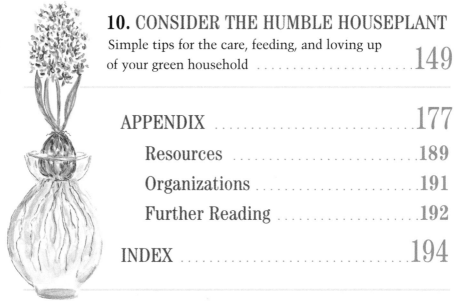

AUTHOR'S NOTE

"May I a small house and large garden have;

And a few friends,

And many books, both true."

—Abraham Cowley

"Some people always do things standing up in a hammock," was how my friend Ed Reppert described people who seem to learn everything the hard way. I often think the hard way is the ONLY way I ever learn—everything by trial (or trowel) and error. Although I began gardening when I was just a tyke, and studied botany and horticulture for years, it was always by doing and redoing that I learned best.

For over twenty years, I faithfully recorded in my journals sad and happy tales of garden woes, triumphs, mistakes, and the secrets and shortcuts of the hundreds of gardeners who stay in touch with me. Recording things isn't all I do. Every day I test recipes and cures and observe the behavior of birds, insects, reptiles, amphibians, and anything else that stumbles onto my plot of ground.

Anyone walking into my potting area is liable to find four or five mixtures of fertilizer brews and oddball pest blends fermenting and marinating in tubs, strange collections of tools, and cooking utensils hanging everywhere. It is not the aftermath of some cataclysmic natural disaster; it is my laboratory, my living library, and the makings for this book.

Three years ago I devoted my "Heart's Ease" column in *Country Living GARDENER* to a subject entitled "Helpful Hints from an Eccentric Gardener." The column contained an assortment of hints and recipes gleaned from my journals, and the enthusiastic response to the collection gave birth to this, my fourth book-child, *Trowel & Error.*

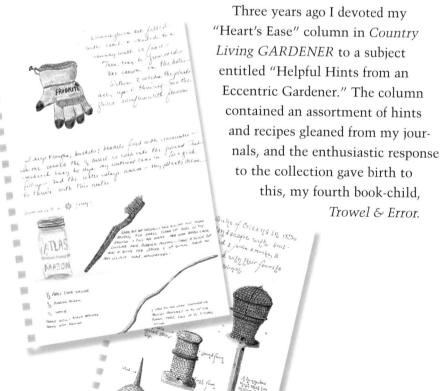

INTRODUCTION

One of my greatest joys is an early-morning walk in the garden. Rain or shine, you'll find me outdoors (usually still in my nightgown), surveying the condition of my plants. I scan the beds and container gardens in search of yellowed leaves, stunted or deformed foliage—anything out of the ordinary that points to disease or an infestation. It would be as difficult for me to overlook a sick plant as it would have been for me not to notice my son Noah's face speckled with bright, red measles.

My friend and garden assistant Peggy tells me that of all the yards she helps tend, mine is the healthiest (although it is not necessarily the tidiest). I credit that health to a myriad of factors. First, every speck of my growing areas (even potted plants) is covered with aged compost, worm castings, finely chipped bark, or shredded leaves and pine needles.

A major part of my garden success is a result of purchasing healthy, thriving plants, bulbs, and bare root specimens. I scrutinize everything for pests, from soil to roots, stems to foliage, before introducing a new plant into my garden.

After giving my new additions a stringent health inspection, I make sure to plant them in an area that suits their needs—for example, sunflowers in full sun, camellias in dappled shade. A plant located in the right environment, with good soil and a dependable supply of water, will thrive and remain healthy.

I believe in planting a diverse array of bulbs, annuals, perennials, shrubs, and trees throughout the landscape. I think of this approach as a healthy layer cake, from the tiniest creeping thymes to the loftiest redwoods, oaks, and cedars. My well-integrated garden provides a multifaceted environment that attracts scores of beneficial inhabitants such as insects, lizards, toads, frogs, snakes, and birds. Working together, this troupe of creatures attacks, parasitizes, and consumes pest populations that might flourish and destroy a less-diversified garden.

The shelves in my potting shed will never hold ingredients bearing the suffix "-cide," from the Latin *caedo*, "to kill." Pesticides, fungicides, insecticides, herbicides, and rodenticides are composed of dangerous chemicals with fatal and far-reaching effects on the earth. Another popular pest control I avoid is Bt (*Bacillus thuringiensis*), a bacterium that kills most caterpillars, including beneficial butterflies and moths. Hand-picking or spraying with

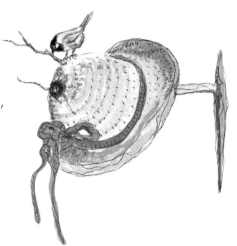

nontoxic potions works just fine for me, and is no more time-consuming than the application of Bt.

In the end, I believe that my morning walks (and talks) with the hundreds of plants and trees are what keep my garden healthy. Not much escapes my notice and immediate attention, and a quick response can mean the difference between the beginning of a small problem and a full-blown attack or infection.

Go outside today (pajamas permitted) and visit with your plants. Just a few minutes of this quiet time of reflection and inspection can change the way you look at and tend your garden. You will begin to discover not only problems, but also the small miracles (often overlooked) quietly unfurling, blooming, and hatching everywhere around you. Cultivate wonder in your garden, and expect the unexpected.

Outdoor

PART ONE

GARDENING

...LOVEJOY'S BEST TIPS...

Don't be afraid

to break the rules about what to use

for garden tools!

Tricks & Tools
THAT BEND THE RULES

Years ago, I learned that whatever oddball tool or container I wanted to use in the garden was invariably somewhere else, so I determined to outfit my work area with everything I needed, and more. Now my potting shed sports a motley assortment of tools, and more culinary equipment than you'll find in my kitchen. From the ceiling hang baskets, hanks of raffia, and an array of old galvanized tinware. Shelves bow under the weight of rescued and recycled treasures that now help to simplify and enrich my days in the garden.

Cleanup

To remove salt residue from crusty pots and to clean dirty tools, scrub with a mixture of ⅓ white vinegar, ⅓ rubbing alcohol, and ⅓ water. Worn-out

toothbrushes make great scrubbers for small cleanup tasks.

Tool

Attach a soap dish with soap and a nail brush to the side of your potting bench. Dig your finger-nails into the soap before you begin working in the garden.

Old serving pieces—ladles, knives, spoons, and forks—to use as digging and transplanting tools.

Wire whisks or an old egg-beater to whip up your home-brewed bug potions and fertilizers.

A paper-towel dispenser mounted near your work area means you'll always have towels for quick and easy cleanups.

An apple corer makes a miniature dibber for tiny bulbs like muscari, galanthus, and leucojum.

Kitchen or barbecue tongs for picking up offensive things like slugs and pulling up stinging nettles.

Shelf

Grapefruit knives, with their sharp, curved blades, make perfect weeders for container gardens. They're also great for transplanting seedlings.

Long-handled wooden spoons or spatulas for bouncing bugs off plants (see page 43) and for mixing batches of compost tea, potting soils, and fertilizers.

Attach brass cup hooks to your potting bench for hanging measuring cups and spoons.

Old colanders or laundry baskets for harvesting fruits and vegetables.

Heavy-duty paper clips and clothespins have hundreds of uses in your work area—from sealing opened seed packets to clipping gloves closed as a precaution against spiders.

Oil Jobs

Fill a used lotion or hand-soap dispenser bottle with mineral oil. Squirt the oil onto metal tools every time you use them, or any time you need to remove sticky sap, grime, or sawdust. Then wipe tools with fine steel wool.

To keep your string trimmer from breaking or sticking, coat the line with mineral oil or spray with Pam.

Mineral Oil
for my tools

> "The purpose of a garden is to give its owner the best and highest kind of earthly pleasure."
>
> —Gertrude Jekyll

PINUPS

HANG OLD CLOTHESPINS along a wire. When harvesting herbs, garlic, onions, and flowers, use the pins to sort and clip them into bunches.

Keep a basket of clothespins and pieces of string in your garden for shoring up sagging plants on trellises or giving a climbing vine a little support.

PICTURE THIS

INSTEAD OF TOSSING OUT that extra wall calendar, take it apart and laminate the page for each month. Attach it (along with a Magic Marker on a string) near your outdoor work area. The more accessible it is, the more you'll use it. For each month, record daily weather and rainfall, and note when seeds sprout, pests appear, bushes bloom, and vegetables ripen. Save all the pages for reference next year.

Snap photos of plantings and borders in each season and clip them onto your laminated calendar or to pages in your journal. Refer to them to refresh your memory about successful color or plant combinations (and the unsuccessful ones, too).

An old calendar lives another year

When faced with the dilemma of what to prune from a tree, take a picture and make a few copies. Then, with correction fluid, block out branches you want to cut and you'll be able to see exactly how your tree will look.

CHART THE SUN

DRAW A SKETCH of your yard, and make several copies. Observe your site morning, noon, and afternoon during the growing season, and use colored markers to indicate shady and sunny areas. Clip the charts to your calendar or journal and consult them before planting.

RECYCLED FLATS

ASK YOUR NURSERY to save plastic basket-weave flats (18 inches by 18 inches) for you. Use them as compost screeners and as covers to protect emerging seedlings. Or line them with newspaper, fill with soil, and plant your own seedlings in them. They're also great for drying flowers and herbs.

Reading Your Landscape

LEGEND	
Full Sun	
Dappled Shade	
Deep Shade	

STRAWBERRY BASKETS

RECYCLE THOSE PLASTIC strawberry or tomato baskets as cloches for tender young plants and bulbs or as organizing tools for your seed packets.

Line the little baskets with brown paper bags, newspaper, or paper towels, add soil, and plant them with the seeds of finicky flowers and vegetables that don't like to be transplanted. Once a set of true leaves (see "True Leaves" on page 96) appears, tuck the baskets directly into the ground and the roots will find their way out.

SOCK IT TO 'EM

GIVE NEW LIFE to mateless or holey, old socks. Cut the foot off and slip the uppers over your wrists to protect your arms from small cuts and your shirts from dirt and damage. They're especially good when you're working around berries and roses.

Slip clean socks or nylons over ripening fruits you want to protect from hungry pests. Remember to remove the socks a few days before harvest so the fruit can color.

UPSTANDING SOLUTIONS

Transform a holey watering can into a twine dispenser. Remove the watering head, place a ball of twine inside, and draw the twine through the spout. Keep a pair of scissors tied to the handle for easy use.

Keep bunches of long twigs and pea stakes in sand-filled buckets stationed throughout your garden. Use them to trellis or stake your plants and enjoy them as free-form garden sculpture.

Store a roll of string inside an upside-down terra-cotta pot and pull the string end through the hole.

For a pocket twine dispenser, use a grated-cheese container, and run the twine through a hole in the lid.

Hang a role of Velcro tape on a nail. Use the Velcro for quick and easy adjustable tie-ups of vines, shrubs, and veggies.

Grow your own bamboo plant supports in a large half-barrel filled with potting soil. Check with your local nursery for species that grow well in your area. The running bamboos are hardy and thrive in cramped quarters. You'll be surprised how quickly a grove will fill a barrel!

Use concrete reinforcing wire (found in lumber yards) as a trellis or arbor, or bend the wire into the shape of a tunnel.

Harvest Helper

Harvest fruits and vegetables in old colanders or laundry baskets and wash them outdoors. You'll save yourself lots of cleanup mess indoors.

These sturdy and inexpensive supports quickly take on a rusty, antique look that blends beautifully into a garden.

GOING TO POT

🦋 Inexpensive bushel baskets make rustic planters for potatoes and tomatoes.

🦋 Commandeer discarded wooden produce boxes (your grocer is usually delighted to give these away) and plant them with mini-vegetables.

🦋 Use scraps of that ubiquitous bubble wrap to insulate the inside walls of thin plastic and metal plant containers to prevent the harmful buildup of heat. Line the sides of your containers before filling them with soil.

🦋 Turn an old wheelbarrow into a movable garden. Plant an ever-changing array of perennials or a medley of herbs, and move it to follow the sun.

🦋 Create an instant raised planter for espaliered trees and specimen bushes. Remove a few portions of the bottom of an old half-barrel (not all, or the barrel will collapse), and set it in place. Fill the barrel with good soil and compost, and plant your tree.

The roots will roam freely once they reach the ground. Fertilize trees monthly.

SCREEN SAVERS

CUT AN OLD SCREEN or panty hose into small squares and use the squares to cover drainage holes in containers. The screen keeps soil from washing out and critters from getting in. (Slugs, earwigs, and pillbugs can get through pebbles or shards.)

PLAYING CHOPSTICKS

🦋 Stockpile the chopsticks that come with Chinese take-out and use them as dibbers for planting small bulbs.

🦋 Become adept at using chopsticks to pick up slugs and other gross interlopers, and dispose of them in soapy water.

🦋 Two chopsticks stuck into the ground at an angle act as an anchor for lightweight strawberry basket cloches.

🦋 Wire copper plant labels to chopsticks and set them firmly in the ground.

Measuring Up

Paint inch and foot marks on the wooden handles of hoes, shovels, and rakes. Use these whenever you need to measure in the garden—for example, when spacing transplants or seeds.

On the Rocks

Famed gardener Gertrude Jekyll felt that the best plant markers were flat river stones lettered with plant names.

PLANT LABELS

🦋 Cut miniblinds or old wooden venetian blinds into short lengths and label them with acrylic paint or a waterproof pen.

🦋 Laminate seed packets and then glue them to tongue depressors or Popsicle sticks for informational garden markers.

🦋 Old slate roof tiles or contemporary slate floor tiles make enduring markers. Use acrylic paint to print the name, then stick the slate about 2 inches into the ground. Use a masonry blade to cut larger tiles.

🦋 For tiny labels, write the plant names on tongue depressors.

L'EAU CHAUD

MANY FRENCH PROVENÇAL gardeners set old half-barrels throughout their gardens to catch rainwater. The proximity of the barrels to their work areas makes hand-watering with a can easier, and they believe warm water is best for plants.

STEPPING UP AND OUT

PROP AN OLD wooden ladder (past its prime for safe use) against a wall to serve as a trellis. Plant pumpkins, gourds, or squash at its feet.

Lay an old ladder flat on the ground and fill the spaces between the steps with soil to create raised beds—perfect for herbs, an array of lettuces, or flowers.

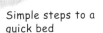

Simple steps to a quick bed

UNDER COVER

PLASTIC AND TERRA-COTTA pots turned upside down make great cloches and blanching pots.

BUG SLED

PUT THAT SNOW SLED to new use in the spring. Tape a piece of cardboard over the seat, allowing it to hang over the sides. Apply Stickum Goo (see recipe, page 40) onto the sides and top of the cardboard. Pull the sled over your beds, straddling your crops of small seedlings. As pests leap out of the way, they get stuck dead in their tracks.

Instant Pond

Turn a trash can lid upside down and bury it in the ground up to the rim. Place a layer of pebbles inside, and fill with water.

HOLD-ALLS

GARDENERS CAN NEVER have too many trash cans in their work areas—they can hold mulch, worm castings, fertilizer, and organic compost teas.

GET A GRIP

SLIP A SCRAP OF FOAM RUBBER pipe insulation over tool handles for a better grip.

NEW FRUIT IN OLD BOTTLES

GIVE NEW LIFE to those beautiful bottles you can't bear to toss. Clean and sterilize them, then check your pear, apple, peach, or nectarine trees for any tiny, unblemished fruit that's forming. Gently slip the attached fruit through the mouth of the bottle and make a sling with cheesecloth or old panty hose to cradle the bottle from an overhanging branch. Tuck plastic in neck to keep out water. When the fruit matures, snip the branch, remove the sling, and fill the bottle with brandy. Cork it tightly, and after about six months, serve as a flavored liqueur.

BROWN-BAG LAUNCH

UNEARTH THAT STASH of paper bags—you know, the one you've been hoarding for years—and turn the bags into planters. Spray or brush the inside of the bags with canola oil, let them air-dry, then fill them with soil and plant your seeds. Morning glories, moon vines, gourds, and many other plants don't like to be transplanted, so when it's time to transplant into your garden, leave the seedlings in the bags and plant them directly in the soil. The bags will eventually decompose as the plants take root.

Enclose young apples in small brown paper bags to protect them from pecking birds and hungry insects. When the fruits are still small, slit the bottom of a bag, slip the fruit in, and staple the top closed. Remove the bag a few days before harvesting so the apples can color.

SUPPORT HOSE

MAKE A HOSE GUIDE with two terra-cotta pots. Place the bottom pot upside down at the corner of a flower bed that you want to protect from the dragging hose. Stack the other pot right side up on top of the first one. Push a dowel through the drainage holes to anchor the pots to the ground.

Alternatively, pound pairs of stakes a hose-width apart at each corner of the bed, and lay the hose between the stakes.

Homely but Useful

Don't toss that bleach bottle with a handle. When it's empty, just rinse it thoroughly, trim the bottom, and voilà! it's a heavy-duty garden scooper.

VICTORIAN BLANCHING COLLARS

IT WORKED FOR Victorian gardeners, and it still can't be beat for blanching leeks, endive, and chicory. Make "collars" by slitting one side of a brown bag, then spray the interior with cooking oil. Turn the bag upside down over the plant, and bury it about 1 inch in the soil. Loosely tie at top and bottom with twine, and bank the soil against the bag to hold it in place.

HIT THE MILK BOTTLE

CUT OFF THE BOTTOM of a plastic milk bottle, and slip the top (cloche-style) over a tender plant that needs protection from cold or animals. Remember to remove the cap so that heat will not build up during the day. You can use the bottom as a platform to keep melons, squash, and cucumbers off the ground.

No water is wasted.

Poke small drainage holes in a gallon milk container and bury it, with the neck exposed, beside a plant that requires extra irrigation. When you're making your daily rounds, fill the container with water. Moisture will slowly leak through the holes and keep the plant hydrated.

WHEELED HELPERS

IF YOU'RE LUCKY, you might find a wooden splint market basket at a flea market or antique store. The tall sides and wheels make it a cinch to transport rakes, shovels, and spades. Some gardeners prefer old golf carts with all their pockets and pouches, but for charm you can't improve on a basket cart.

Wooden splint basket cart for hauling tools.

Borrow your child's little red wagon (the ones with the high wooden sides are nifty) for hauling heavy bags of soil, rocks, and tools.

WORM WAGON

USE A HOLEY OLD RED WAGON as a traveling "worm wagon." Spread a piece of screen across the floor of the wagon so the worms don't escape. Scoop in a few piles of worms and castings. Add soil and some juicy garbage, such as lettuce leaves, top with more soil, water thoroughly,

> "I have several acres about my house, which I call my garden, and which a skillful gardener would not know what to call."
>
> —Joseph Addison, 1712

and cover the whole creation with a piece of plywood. Move the wagon around your yard to areas that need the nutritious worm water that flows through the holes and onto the soil. And wherever you have containers that need toppings, just scoop out some wonderful wormy soil.

FRIEND AND FAUX

SNIP A WORN-OUT black or dark green hose into 3-foot sections and paint the hose with patterns to resemble snakeskins. Drape the hose over tree branches to keep squirrels, raccoons, and birds away from your fruit.

SOLAR HEATER

SURROUND A YOUNG heat-loving plant with a wall of water-filled bottles, which block the wind, warm the air around the plant, and radiate heat into the soil.

GARDENER'S HELPERS

🦋 Broad concrete finishing trowels, called Fresno trowels, are perfect for pressing newly sown seeds into a flower bed.

🦋 Glue a small mirror onto a yardstick to check the undersides of leaves for pests. Ideal for a gardener who has trouble bending over.

🦋 You might think a bucket with holes in it is useless, but it's not. Fill the bucket with water and hang it on a tree limb over a large terra-cotta saucer. The steady drip of water attracts songbirds that bathe in the saucer, and sweet woodruff and Corsican mint thrive in the moist areas surrounding it.

🦋 Turn your spade into an extra pair of hands. Whenever you need to direct a flow of water onto a portion of your garden, simply stick the tool into the soil and nestle your hose into the V-shaped notch where the handle begins.

🦋 Tin cans with lids can be used as perches for melons and squash,

A spade makes a handy sprinkler stand.

Car Potpourri

Whenever you need to dry flowers or herbs quickly, look no further than your car! Cover flat surfaces with paper, spread a layer of fragrant blooms, close the windows, and park in the sun.

and cans without lids serve as protective housing for cylindrical veggies such as zucchinis and cucumbers.

🦋 Save old coffee cans and their plastic lids for yard cleanup. As you snip diseased leaves off plants (especially important for rust), place the leaves in the can, close the lid, and dispose of the leaves in the trash. To stop the spread of rust, don't compost them. Rust spores travel through the air and enter the stomata in leaves.

🦋 When you clean your pond, toss the nutrient-rich algae and scummy water onto the soil around your plants. It's great fertilizer.

🦋 When working around a staked plant, avoid accidental injury by placing a piece of cork on the tip of the stake.

🦋 Follow the old-fashioned practice of using "backing boards" to reflect light onto vines and other sun-loving plants. Cover a board with aluminum foil or any reflective metal, prop it against a rock, and aim it toward sun worshippers such as tomatoes, peppers, or eggplants.

Measuring cups

Tool on hook

Cloches

Extra hose

Recessed tub of soil

Trash cans for compost
& liquid fertilizer

Worm castings

Winnower

Twine inside pot

The tools of a gardener's trade

🦋 Hasten the ripening of squash and melons by slicing flat stepping-stones or pieces of broken concrete underneath the produce. The stones trap heat and protect the crop from rotting on the ground.

🦋 Control invasive horseradish plants, and coax them into putting down long, straight roots, by planting them in galvanized vent pipe. Set the pipe vertically up to the rim in a predug hole. Fill the pipe with good potting soil, slide in the horseradish, and tamp down the soil.

Don't be afraid to break the rules about what to use for garden tools!

...LOVEJOY'S BEST TIPS...

Spot-test potions

before every spray,

So your plants will survive

and pests go away.

....

CHAPTER

2

Potions

In tackling the problems of pests and disease, I always turn to the most benign and natural forms of control. Simple methods that involve minimal materials are very often effective: hand-pick or vacuum invaders and drop them into a bucket of soapy water; set up barriers or lures to thwart or capture critters; or simply trim off problem areas and dispose of the contaminated foliage. If these interventions fail, I apply my simple, tested homemade potions to treat my gardens, always keeping in mind the welfare of the soil and the dwellers who share the earth with me.

The Indispensable Dispensary

LIKE A WELL-STOCKED PANTRY for a cook, a good arsenal of supplies will save a gardener oodles of time and money. Most of these products are things you already have at home in your bathroom medicine cabinet or kitchen pantry. Some can be used alone; others are mixed with things like liquid soap or oil into potable plant potions that treat almost every gardening woe. Store these ingredients in a handy location—and out of children's reach.

Boric acid or borax—wipes out ants, roaches, and more.

Canola oil—use to smother insects and as a surfactant.

Castor oil—repels moles.

Chili powder—pesticide and repellent.

Cinnamon powder—antifungal and anti-ant.

Corn gluten meal—inhibits germination of weeds.

Aspirin (uncoated)—dissolved in water, fights mildew, black spot, and more.

Baking soda (and potassium bicarbonate)—prevents fungus spores from invading plants.

Epsom salts—provide a quick shot of magnesium and promote growth of flowers and foliage.

Essential oils (mixed with water)—antifeedant and pest buster.

Fermented salmon—thwarts deer, chipmunks, and other critters, and is rich with micronutrients, amino acids, fatty acids, and vitamins.

Fish emulsion and **kelp** (liquid or powder)—natural organic fertilizers that promote healthy soil and plants.

Flour (white, but not self-rising)—for sprinkling on plants plagued by grasshoppers.

Honey—a lure for ants.

Isopropyl rubbing alcohol (70 percent solution)—desiccates and destroys insects.

Molasses (blackstrap or horticultural grade)—jump-starts microbial action, feeds beneficial insects, and attracts harmful insects to traps.

Petroleum jelly (or mentholated rub)—a sticky barrier to apply to trunks and stems and onto lures.

Liquid soap (Dr. Bronner's, Fels Naphtha, or any pure castile soap)—available in health food stores.

Tabasco® sauce—pesticide and repellent.

Vegetable or mineral oil—destroys insect pests and can be used as a physical barrier.

Vinegar (apple cider and white)—fights fungus gnats, kills weeds, and destroys pests.

White glue—seals small pruning cuts (especially good for roses).

Why Soap?

Liquid soap is the basis of many "potions" here because it allows other ingredients to emulsify or blend together. It's also a surfactant, or wetting agent, which means it will assure uniform coverage of leaf surfaces or insect bodies. I recommend dumping insect pests into a bucket of soapy water because the soap will penetrate the waxy insect body and cause desiccation and death.

Diatomaceous Earth

These fossilized, silica shell remains of prehistoric diatoms make an abrasive barrier, and desiccate insect bodies. Always purchase *natural* diatomaceous earth, which is mined, ground, and sifted. (Swimming-pool grade contains crystalline silica, a respiratory hazard.)

SPRAYING TIPS

🦋 Test homemade sprays on a small portion of the plant before applying it to the entire surface. Monitor the plant's response for a couple of days to check for burning.

🦋 Always use soap (never detergent) so as not to burn plants.

🦋 Prevent sunburned leaves by applying sprays early in the morning, and never when the temperature is above 85 degrees.

🦋 Wear rubber gloves when using any sprays containing peppers, alcohol, citrus concentrates, mint oils, or anything else that could irritate your skin. And when spraying outdoors in breezy conditions, wear eye and nose protection.

🦋 Thoroughly examine your plants before applying sprays to make sure that you aren't spraying any spiders or beetles that might be your allies in the fight against pests.

BOOSTERS

BOOSTER SHOT

WHEN YOUR TOMATOES, eggplants, and peppers begin to bloom, mix up a batch of this potent potion to encourage prolific, healthy fruiting. Pour onto the soil surrounding your plants.

> **2 TABLESPOONS EPSOM SALTS**
>
> **1 GALLON WATER**

The magnesium and sulfur in the Epsom salts are macronutrients that foster fruiting.

CALCIUM BOOSTER

WHENEVER YOU'RE at the seashore, collect a few empty crab shells (they are rich in both calcium and chitin), and tote them home for your tomatoes. Crush them thoroughly between two sheets of wax paper and work the fragments into the soil surrounding the tomatoes.

Why Oil?

A foliar application of vegetable or mineral oil mixed with an emulsifier (soap) will destroy insect pests and smother their eggs. Oil coats leaves, binding and holding ingredients in place. A thin layer of oil forms a physical barrier that stops pests and hinders the formation of fungus.

KELP COCKTAIL

IF YOU LIVE CLOSE to the seashore, you have access to an unlimited supply of one of the best plant foods and mulches available—kelp. It contains more than sixty minerals, potassium, and cytokinins that stimulate both growth and flower formation. Make a Kelp Cocktail by substituting kelp for compost in the recipe for Container Champagne (below). You can also use pieces of well-rinsed kelp as a mulch (potatoes benefit especially).

FIGHT FROST DAMAGE

TO CUT DOWN ON frost damage, spray Kelp Cocktail on plants before a predicted frost. It increases the plant's sugar content which lowers the freezing point.

KELP FOR HEALTHY APPLES

TO IMPROVE BUD hardiness and increase fruit set, apply a monthly foliar application of kelp until the fruit is set.

CONTAINER CHAMPAGNE

NUTRIENTS ARE QUICKLY leached through the soil of container plants. Nurture both the soil and the plants with this simple but powerful drink.

Fill an old pillowcase or mesh bag with finished compost or manure and soak in a trash can filled with water. Add a pound of blackstrap molasses to kick-start the microbial activity, stir, and cover.

Let the blend age for ten days. Remove the pillowcase, and use the liquid blend for watering container plants.

SPRING SPRINKLE

STORE CLEAN, COOL wood ashes in a covered trash can. In early spring, mix 4 dry gallons of ash with ½ cup Epsom salts and sprinkle ½ pound of the dry mixture per 100 square feet of soil around your wakening bulbs. Apply only once a year. Wood ash contains calcium (35 percent), phosphorous, and potassium. Epsom salts are high in sulfur (13 percent) and magnesium (10 percent), which are rapidly utilized by plants.

SNIP IT!

COMFREY IS RICH in potassium and nitrogen, two essential ingredients for healthy plants. Snip a few handfuls, put them in a mesh bag, and drop the bag into a large can of water. Add a pound of blackstrap molasses and allow the ingredients to brew for at least ten days. Use this blend to water plants, especially those in containers.

"Gardens are not made by singing 'Oh how beautiful' and sitting in the shade."

—Rudyard Kipling

For acid-loving plants, such as camellias, azaleas, citrus, and heathers, vary the recipe by adding oak leaves and/or pine needles to boost the acid content of the water.

CIAO BUGS!

BASIL SUN TEA

BASIL FIGHTS HARMFUL LEAF HOPPERS, aphids, cabbage loopers, mites, and cucumber beetles, a yellowish-green ladybird beetle lookalike.

Cucumber beetle

Gather a handful of fresh basil leaves and stems, crush them slightly, and stuff them into a large glass jar (at least ½ gallon) filled with water. Cap the jar and set in the sun to brew for a few days. Strain out the solids and store in a covered container until needed as an insecticide. When you're ready to do battle, add to ⅛ teaspoon liquid soap in a spray bottle and shake well before using.

Fino verde basil is fancy and functional.

MOLASSES BATH

FIGHT INFESTATIONS of harmful nematodes and jump-start microbial activity in your soil with an application of blackstrap molasses and water. Add 12½ ounces blackstrap molasses to a gallon of water. Steep for seven to ten days. Pour onto the soil around plants or use as a foliar spray to attract beneficial insects that will prey on harmful pests.

SAUCY SPRAY

TREAT CUCUMBER BEETLES, leaf hoppers, aphids—you name the pest—with a peppery spray made with Tabasco sauce. (See recipe at right.)

Also use Tabasco to dissuade raccoons and rabbits from nibbling tender shoots.

HOT SHOT

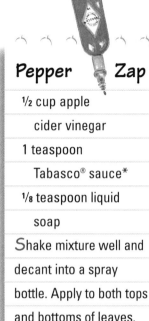

I'VE BEEN USING red pepper for years on everything from cucumber beetles and spittle bugs to leaf hoppers and cabbage loopers. Now there's scientific authority behind this treatment: entomologist Dr. Geoff Zehnder of Auburn University credits McCormick red pepper for protecting cabbages better than any standard chemical insecticide. Mix the following ingredients:

2 TABLESPOONS RED PEPPER

6 DROPS LIQUID SOAP

1 GALLON WATER

Let sit overnight, and stir thoroughly. Spray weekly to protect all members of the cabbage family, including broccoli, cauliflower, kale, and brussels sprouts, from destructive critters.

Pepper Zap

½ cup apple cider vinegar

1 teaspoon Tabasco® sauce*

⅛ teaspoon liquid soap

Shake mixture well and decant into a spray bottle. Apply to both tops and bottoms of leaves.

*As an alternative to Tabasco, use rotting garden produce—mushy tomatoes, peppers, moldy onions. Chop coarsely, puree in a blender, and add.

Homemade Orange Spritzer

Add a few drops of essential oil of orange and a few drops of soap to a 32-ounce spray bottle filled with water. Shake before each use and spray directly on pests.

ORANGE AID

YOU CAN NOW BUY safe, earth-friendly orange cleaning products that are made with plant-derived orange oil and biodegradable surfactants. Citrus contains limonene and linalool, which are contact poisons for aphids, fleas, mites, fire ants, fruit and houseflies, and mealy bugs. Many gardeners use these products to attack pests both indoors and out. Try Seventh Generation's Heavy Duty Citrus Cleaner and Degreaser spray, which can be used straight from the bottle. Another product, Citra-Solv cleaner, is highly concentrated and can burn plants. *Use it only after diluting:* ⅛ teaspoon in 1 quart of water.

BEETLE BUSTER

THROW A HANDFUL of larkspur or delphinium leaves into a blender, add to a gallon of water, and spray on plants attacked by Japanese beetles. The alkaloids in the leaves— deliosine and delsoline—will zap the beetles. Know when the beetles are apt to appear in your garden and spray plants with Surround At Home (see page 68) about two weeks before you expect them.

Japanese beetle

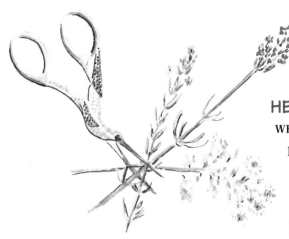

HERBAL BREW

WHEN YOU TRIM HERBS, especially potently scented ones such as lavender, rosemary, tansy, southernwood, rue, mint, wormwood, basil, or sage (a mixture is fine), drop small pieces in a gallon bucket of water and let the mixture sit in the sun for a week.

Add 2 tablespoons of liquid soap to the strained brew and decant into a spray bottle. Keep in a cool, dark storage area. Use on aphids, cucumber beetles, cabbage loopers, and other pests.

AWAKEN YOUR BEDS

SPRAY AN AWAKENING bed of asparagus with a mixture of 5 ounces sugar and 1 tablespoon yeast in 1 quart of water to feed the soil and attract beneficial insects that do battle with the injurious asparagus beetle.

BUTTERMILK SHAKE

SCIENTISTS AT PURDUE University have developed a buttermilk spray to fight spider mites. It can be used whenever a daily spray of plain water doesn't work.

> ¼ CUP BUTTERMILK
>
> 2 CUPS WHEAT FLOUR
>
> 2½ GALLONS WATER

Shake ingredients thoroughly and spray on plants.

Whack garlic with a
can of soup to remove
the skin.

GARLIC SOUP

FOR PESTS OR PLANTS with fungal, viral, and
bacterial diseases, use this simple recipe:

> **2** GARLIC CLOVES
>
> **1** QUART WATER
>
> $\frac{1}{8}$ TEASPOON LIQUID SOAP

Puree garlic in a blender on high for a minute.
Slowly add water, and continue blending for
about 6 minutes. Strain, and add the soap. Pour
the liquid into a storage container. Cover tightly.

When needed, mix 1 part Garlic Soup with
10 parts water in a spray bottle. Scientists have
discovered that the strappy green garlic leaves
are potent in their own right, so you can also
puree two handfuls of leaves instead of using
the bulb.

MAGGOT MARTINI

MIX 1 PART MOLASSES with 10 parts water.
Add a sprinkling of yeast. Pour the mixture into
small vials wrapped with wire holders, and hang
the vials in the lower branches on the sunny
side of apple trees. Maggots can't resist, and will
leap like the proverbial lemmings to their death.
Empty the vials when they're full and replace
the mixture after rain.

DISEASE FIGHTERS

HEALTHY HOLLYHOCK SPRAY

FOR RUST-FREE hollyhocks and roses, use this spray. It also treats black spot.

$1^1\!/_2$ **TEASPOONS BAKING SODA**

1 TABLESPOON CANOLA OIL

$^1\!/_2$ **TEASPOON SOAP**

$^1\!/_2$ **CUP WHITE VINEGAR**

1 GALLON WATER

Blend ingredients and pour into a spray bottle. Shake thoroughly before each use, and apply weekly to tops and bottoms of leaves. Always remove diseased foliage, and dispose of it in a trash can (do *not* compost).

CHAMOMILE TEA

HALT DAMPING-OFF, a fungal disease that strikes indoor-started seedlings, by watering them from the bottom with this simple brew.

16 CHAMOMILE TEA BAGS (OR **2** CUPS DRIED CHAMOMILE FLOWERS)

2 QUARTS WATER

Simmer gently for 20 minutes, then turn off heat and allow tea bags to remain in the water for several hours. Strain, if using flowers, and water the plants at the roots. Spray foliage with the tea daily until transplanted outdoors.

TREE, TREAT THYSELF

ANDY LOPEZ, founder of Invisible Gardeners, as well as pathologists in British Columbia, found that the bark and leaves of healthy trees can be used to treat sick trees (oozing sores or cankers on peach, cherry, apricot, and plum) and can inoculate healthy trees against infection.

Take enough bark and/or leaves from the branch of a healthy tree (willow leaves work especially well) to stuff a sock. Let the sock "tea bag" steep in 3 gallons of water for at least 24 hours, then remove. Pour the water into spray bottles and apply to cankers.

THE ASPIRIN SOLUTION

WHEN YOU NOTICE fungus infections—such as black spot, mildew, or rust—attacking your plants, dissolve 2 uncoated aspirin tablets (325 mg) in 1 quart water and use the mixture as a foliar spray.

GOT MILK?

BRAZILIAN AGRONOMIST Wagner Bettiol discovered that a mixture of milk and water cured mildew-infected plants more effectively than toxic fungicides. Scientists have also proven that this milk spray will prevent tomato mosaic.

1 CUP MILK

9 CUPS WATER

Shake well and pour into a spray bottle. Apply to infected plants twice weekly. Refrigerate between use.

CORNELL FORMULA

TOMATOES AND POTATOES are known for their susceptibility to both early and late fungal blights. Spray this proven Cornell University formula on these crops early in their growing season.

1 TABLESPOON CANOLA OR MINERAL OIL

1 TEASPOON BAKING SODA

1 GALLON WATER

Shake thoroughly before each use.

ROSE TONIC

THIS BLEND FOR ROSES with powdery mildew or black spot will remain effective for months.

2 TEASPOONS BAKING SODA

2 QUARTS WATER

½ TEASPOON LIQUID SOAP
   OR MURPHY'S OIL SOAP

Keep a spray bottle filled and ready to do battle. Shake well before each use. *Note:* Soap increases the moisture on plant leaves so spores are unable to germinate.

"There ain't nothing better in life than true love and a homegrown tomato."

—Old saying

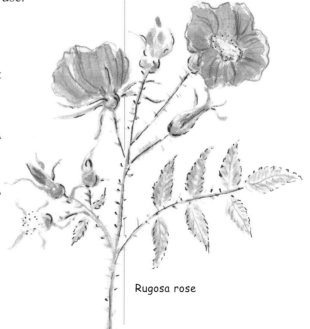

Rugosa rose

Take a Powder

Mix equal amounts garlic powder and diatomaceous earth. Use an old flour sifter (which must forevermore be retired from kitchen duty) to apply this mixture to plants with mildew.

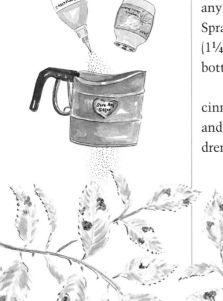

MILDEW CURES

PATCHY GRAY AREAS on top of plant leaves are a sign of powdery mildew. Gray spots under plant leaves indicate debilitating downy mildew. Attack the problem as soon as it appears. The best preventive is to give your plants a shower every hot afternoon. Drenching the leaves removes spores, and the film of water provides a barrier against new spores.

Two homemade potions, one garlic, the other cinnamon, are easy to mix and spray on any leaves afflicted with mildew. For the Garlic Spray, mix 1 gallon water with 20 tablespoons (1¼ cups) of garlic powder. Pour into a spray bottle and apply to plants early in the morning.

For Spicy Cinnamon Spray, mix ¼ teaspoon cinnamon powder in one quart of warm water and pour into a spray bottle. Remember to drench both sides of the leaves thoroughly and early in the day.

Powdery
mildew

STRAW SOLUTION

TO RID A POND of algae, without resorting to harsh chemicals, float small bales of barley straw 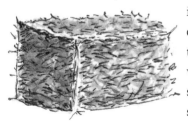 in the water. Use 8 ounces straw per 500 to 1,500 gallons water. Through the season, the barley straw will decompose and release tiny particles of hydrogen peroxide, which stops the growth of algae. Replace with a fresh bale every 4 months.

"It's better to know some of the questions than all of the answers."

—James Thurber

...L O V E J O Y' S   B E S T   T I P S ...

When first you discover

unwanted pests

a strong blast of water

usually works best.

Chapter 3

GETTING THE BEST OF

Pesky Pests

Prowl around in your garden for a few minutes every day to keep in touch with the health of your plants. You'll be surprised how quickly you begin to notice every tattered edge on insect-damaged leaves or the slightest telltale droop of a besieged bush. Awareness and a quick response are two of your best allies against garden foes.

Sometimes it takes only the shake of a branch, a blast of water, or a dusting of diatomaceous earth to rid your plants of pests. Many of the best and most effective cures available are simple, quick, earth-friendly, and fun to make.

APPLE DECOYS

CONFUSE APPLE MAGGOTS with lookalike apple lures tied with yellow plastic bows. Paint apple-sized rubber balls bright red and hang them with fishing line from apple tree branches. Slather the balls with Stickum Goo (see sidebar for recipe) and tie a broad yellow bow at the top. Brush more goo onto the bow. Remove the balls when they become covered with carcasses, clean with hot water, dry, and refresh the gooey jelly.

BURN THE BAD GUYS

INCINERATE INSECT LARVAE and harmful pathogens that overwinter inside fruits and fallen leaves around fruit trees (especially those with noticeable infestations of scab). Use a commercially available, hand-held propane torch to burn the debris as you walk among your fruit trees.

FLOUR POWER

SPRINKLE WHITE FLOUR (*not* self-rising) on cabbage worms, loopers, and grasshoppers early in the morning when the plants are covered with dew. Pests will literally petrify into desiccated little bug cakes. Rinse off the plants the next day.

Stickum Goo

Blend equal parts mineral oil, liquid soap, and petroleum jelly or mentholated rub.

Stick Around

AGITATE YOUR APHIDS

SCIENTISTS AT TEXAS A&M University estimate that up to 90 percent of problems with aphids, mites, and spittlebug nymphs can be cured with water. A strong blast of water dislodges aphids and breaks off their sucking mouth parts.

🦋 Did you know that aphids are irresistibly drawn to the color yellow? Set a shallow, yellow pan of soapy water near your infested plants, and the aphids will plunge to a watery end.

🦋 Order a container of aphid wolves, the larvae of ladybird beetles (see Resources, pages 189–90), and release them into your garden. These hungry predators can eat hundreds of aphids a day.

🦋 Use adhesive tape to remove aphids from plant leaves. Wrap a long piece of tape around your fingers (sticky side out), and blot off the aphids.

Caution: Some readers who tried this say it can become habit-forming.

Allied Forces

Chickens, guinea fowl, tiger beetles, and social wasps are great allies in the war against pests.

Host Trees

Look for bagworms on arborvitae, cypress, hemlock, juniper, spruce, buckeye, elm, maple, sycamore, and willow.

IN THE BAG

PLUCK THOSE DANGLING baggy webs from your trees, and drop them into hot, soapy water. Each bag, which is disguised with bits and pieces of the host tree, contains a female bagworm—a wingless, eyeless, legless mating machine (pretty attractive, huh?). This means the bag probably also contains as many as 2,000 eggs, each of which will turn into another eating machine.

RING AROUND THE ROSES

SOME GARDENERS have had success deterring Japanese beetles by planting a ring of garlic and chives around their rosebushes and potatoes.

JAPANESE BEETLE DANCE

THESE BEAUTIFUL but devastating pests need no introduction. Get rid of them! Invest in the most important and lethal pair of sandals you'll ever own. They're called Lawn Aerator Sandals (see Resources, page 189), and they're one of the best ways to destroy the grubs before they become beetles. After a rain when the grubs surface, slip on a pair of the sandals and dance wildly on your wet lawn.

BUG BOUNCERS

BOUNCE THOSE BUGS right out of your garden with a long-handled spatula or spoon. Go outside early in the morning with your beetle bouncer and a bucket of warm, soapy water.

Look for infestations on roses, peonies, and other favorites. Hold the bucket below the bloom and gently whack the flower. The bugs will drop straight down and into your suds. Reuse the soapy water as a spray.

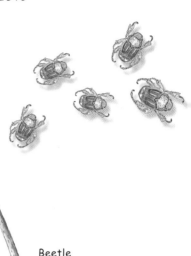

Beetle
bouncer

BEETLES ON THE BEDSHEET

SPREAD A SHEET below foliage infested with cucumber, Japanese, or Colorado potato beetles or squash bugs. Again, go out in the early morning and bounce or shake the insects off the plants and onto the sheet (they'll instinctively drop straight down). Vacuum or shake the contents of the sheet into a bucket of hot, soapy water. You may need to coax the insects with a stiff-bristled brush; they hold on tightly. (I suggest retiring the sheet after use.)

Cucumber and Japanese beetles get trapped in the bag.

FUNNEL AWAY BEETLES AND BUGS

ARM YOURSELF with a large funnel (or make one by cutting off the bottom of a plastic bottle) and attack cucumber and Japanese beetles and squash bugs early in the morning. Tie a bag to the narrow end of the funnel. Slip the wide mouth of the funnel beneath the infested foliage and shake the plant or blossom. The insects will slide down and into the bag. When finished, tie bag closed and drop it into a trash can.

MERCENARY METHODS

Spined soldier bug

PURCHASE SPINED soldier bugs, a beetle's greatest enemy, from an insectary (see Resources, pages 189–90) or nursery and set them on patrol in your garden. Purchase beneficial parasitic nematodes (see Resources), mix with water, and apply to a well-watered lawn.

IT'S A CINCH

SCIENTISTS AT THE Bio-Integral Research Center in Berkeley devised this method to detect and cure the problem of chinch bugs: Mix 1 ounce liquid soap in a 2-gallon bucket of water. Drench a 2-foot square of lawn with the liquid, let sit 2 or 3 minutes, then cover the entire area with a white flannel blanket. In about half an hour, lift the blanket and check for the chinch bugs, which get tangled in the nap. Rinse the buggy material in a bucket of hot, soapy water.

Drench small areas of buggy lawn with the chinch mixture above, and use a shop vacuum to suck up emerging nymphs. Destroy the contents of the shop vacuum in hot, soapy water.

POTATOES ON A STICK

WIREWORMS, the larvae of click beetles, feed

Click beetle

voraciously on root vegetables such as carrots, beets, turnips, potatoes, and bulbs. Cut a potato into pieces, pierce with a stick, and bury a few inches into the soil, with the stick protruding. Every week, pull up the sticks and destroy the wireworm-infested pieces. Rebait as needed.

Fowl Deed

If you keep chickens and don't allow them in your gardens, you're passing up a great source of cheap labor. They pluck weeds and devour potato bugs, larvae, earwigs, grubs, and slugs and turn them into rich chicken manure. Build a bottomless, portable chicken pen, and move it around your garden or lawn where you're having bug problems.

Gypsy moths

 Gardenside First Aid

Rub the fresh leaves of these plants onto your skin and hair to ward off pesky insects: sweet basil, pennyroyal, lemon balm, lemon thyme, orange bergamot mint, peppermint, spearmint, catmint, and Japanese mint.

SNAG GYPSY MOTHS

FOOL GYPSY MOTHS into believing they've found the perfect place to lay their eggs. Fold sticky shelf-lining paper in half, sticky side out, and tape it to a tree. Replace the paper after rain, and scrape the moth egg masses beneath the paper into soapy water.

Or use the method touted by Chinese farmers. Attach 8-inch strips of burlap completely around tree trunks. Moth larvae become snagged in the strips and caterpillars congregate in their shelter. Check the strips daily, and drop the critters into soapy water.

SIMPLE EARWIG TRAPS

FILL AN EMPTY cardboard milk carton with crumpled moist newspaper and bread crumbs, and set on its side in your garden. Or crush newspaper into tight balls, moisten with water, and place among the plants.

Pour equal•parts canola oil and soy sauce into a shallow container and place in infested areas. Each morning arm yourself with a bucket of soapy water, check the lures, and dispose of the victims.

Earwig

COLLARED!

WRAP.CORRUGATED CARDBOARD around the trunks of fruit trees (corrugated side toward the trunk). The larvae of the codling moth will take shelter underneath to pupate. Remove collars weekly and scrape the larvae into hot, soapy water.

Codling moth

ROACH RULES

FIGHT ROACHES with boric acid. Apply this powerful powder in a light coating, because if you make piles or place it in containers, the roaches will shun it. Use a small-tipped plastic squeeze bottle to shoot the dust into cracks and crevices. As the roaches search for food, the fine powder accumulates on their bodies. When they groom themselves—which these supposedly dirty critters do constantly—they ingest the deadly powder. Keep dry and reapply after rains. Store container and boric acid out of reach of pets and children.

Don't Make a Mountain . . .

Moles are often blamed for garden problems, but these insectivores (they have a nearly 100 percent insect diet) can eliminate thousands of grubs and insects weekly. Harvest some of the rich, crumbly soil from their mounds and use it as a great topper for container plants.

Moles help aerate soil.

Ants Begone

nts are good soil aerators and food for birds, lizards, and toads, but if you're determined to eradicate them, use one of these easy solutions:

Cinnamon powder acts as a deterrent for ants. Shake it liberally on black ant trails leading into your home or in other areas where you don't want them.

Spray ant routes with apple cider vinegar to cover their invisible pheromone tracks, so they can't find their way back to their foraging sites.

Fill a shop vacuum with soapy water and suck large concentrations of ants out of their hiding places.

Pour equal parts baking soda and powdered sugar into a bowl and blend thoroughly. Transfer mixture to a cheese or salt shaker and apply directly to ant hills and trails.

Circle an active ant mound with dry cornmeal. Ants feast on the meal, which expands inside them.

I never bother ants, but whenever I see an ant path leading into the house, I fill a salt shaker with white sugar and sprinkle it in an enticing trail AWAY from the house.

Silica aerogel or diatomaceous earth injures the protective cuticle covering on the ant's body and causes desiccation. Shake it into cracks, corners, and holes. Or mix it with sugar and set it out in a peanut butter jar lid.

For plants being farmed by ants, fold sticky shelf-lining paper in half (sticky side out) and strap it around the trunks of fruit trees with duct tape. Change the paper whenever it becomes filled and replace after a rain.

Or set a jar lid of honey at the foot of the tree to attract ants to a sticky demise.

Ant Hotel

Mix 10 teaspoons corn or maple syrup with 1 teaspoon borax. Pour a dab of the mixture into small, lidded plastic containers (plastic film canisters work well). Poke holes in the lid large enough for ants to enter and set the covered containers in areas frequented by ants.

SLUG FEST

SLUGS AND SNAILS are responsible for wiping out many a gardener's dreams. Try some of these successful baits and traps to keep them from your plants.

🦋 Eliminate snail and slug problems by letting a duck roam in your gardens. Ducks are incredible slug and snail hunters, as are toads,

End Wormy Corn

You'll never have to worry about biting into another ear of wormy corn. After the silks turn brown, apply 20 drops of mineral oil to the tips of each ear. Repeat every other day for three weeks. This not only smothers the larvae, but also makes husking a simpler task.

raccoons, firefly glowworms, and decollate snails, which are available from beneficial insect suppliers (see Resources, page 189).

Slugs will collect in empty flowerpots.

🦋 Leave leftover grapefruit and melon rinds in your yard each evening. Scrape the slugs and snails into soapy water every morning. You'll need to put out fresh rinds every few days.

🦋 Water a small portion of your yard in the evening and put down a 1-inch by 12-inch board, elevated slightly on a rock. Early each morning, turn the board over and scrape it clean into soapy water.

Use grapefruit and melon rinds as lures.

🦋 Lay empty flowerpots (or milk cartons) on their sides in a shady area and dispose of slugs and snails every morning.

Sprinkle bran or yeast on cabbage leaves.

🦋 Sprinkle bran or yeast onto cabbage leaves and set in a shaded, moist area. Collect and dispose of leaves daily.

🦋 Sink shallow tubs or saucers into the ground and fill them with cheap beer (slugs and snails aren't too particular) or molasses and a sprinkling of yeast. They dive into it and drown. Empty as needed.

Slugs are drawn to beer for a happy ending.

FIRE ANT BRIGADE

FIRE ANTS are one of the most destructive and dangerous pests found in a garden, causing damage to over fifty species of plants and killing native ants and many species of mammals, reptiles, amphibians, and birds. Their painful sting can cause serious allergic reactions in humans as well.

PREPARE FOR BATTLE

ALWAYS WEAR LONG PANTS, tuck them into your boots, and tie or rubber-band them closed. Dust boots and legs with baby powder or cornstarch to make them slippery. Work quickly and quietly so as not to alert the queen. Plan your attack for a sunny but cool day. Ants will be close to the surface of the mound, and the queen will be on the sunny side.

BATTLE PLANS

NO SINGLE CURE will always work for fire ants, so try a variety of strategies:

Dust the soil around the ant mound with a wide circle of diatomaceous earth. The ants may have foraging tunnels in various areas.

Researchers at Florida State University successfully treated active mounds with boiling water. Use caution, and pour 3 gallons of hot water (194 degrees) onto the mound. Break up crusted soil (before

watering.) Repeat process for three days.

In the winter, attack mounds when temperatures drop to near freezing to expose the ants to cold. Use a broad beam of wood or a landscaping rake to totally level the mound.

BAIT 'N SWITCH

THE BIO-INTEGRAL RESEARCH CEN-TER recommends a sweet bait made of 1 teaspoon boric acid and 10 tea-spoons granulated sugar in 2 cups water. Stir thoroughly and pour into lidded containers pierced with ant-sized entry holes.

Apply the bait during the dry days of spring, summer, and fall. Set cans about 5 feet away from the mounds.

On days over 95 degrees, set your bait can out in the cool evening; lay it on its side in an area where ants forage.

Don't put the cans directly on the mound or the foragers won't find them; place them about 5 feet away.

If water gets into the baits, they won't work. Always keep from children and pets.

Gardenside First Aid

For treatment of fire ant stings, which can cause dangerous anaphylactic reactions in some people, immediately apply a solution of one part bleach to one part water to the affected area and wash thoroughly. If you experience shortness of breath, dizziness, swelling, headache, or sweating, contact your physician.

... L O V E J O Y ' S B E S T T I P S *...*

Outwit your foes

before they appear—

Be they beetles, bunnies,

woodchuck, or deer.

Chapter

Repellents and Preventives

"The first rule is to keep an untroubled spirit.
The second is to look things in the face and know them for what they are."

—Marcus Aurelius

The old adage, "Know thine enemies," is especially important in the garden. By understanding pests, knowing when they arrive or hatch (see Calendar, page 4) where they like to hide, or what plants most attract them, a gardener can remain at least a few strides ahead of them. Often, just a dusting of baby powder, a sleeve of tinfoil, or a mulch of fresh hair clippings is enough to deter foes and save your harvest.

CAN COLLARS

SAVE SMALL TIN or aluminum cans to use as long-lasting cutworm collars. Remove the top and bottom lids and labels, wash the can, and sink it at least 1 inch into the soil. Plant seeds or place seedlings in the center of the can. Keep the inside of the collar free of debris. Sprinkle a ring of cornmeal around the outside of the collar. This is the last supper for cutworms (they feed on it but they can't digest it).

UNDERGROUND WALL

NEMATODES AND CUTWORMS work their underground havoc just a few inches below the surface and are stumped when they run into a wall of plastic. Clean and disinfect old 1- and 5-gallon plastic nursery pots and cut out the bottoms. Sink the pots into the ground, leaving 2 to 3 inches above the soil line. Plant inside them.

STINK-AWAY

STOP CHIPMUNKS from destroying or stealing your sunflowers and tiny tomatoes by

spraying these crops with Coast of Maine
Fermented Salmon (see Resources, page 189).

INVISIBLE LINES

SPREAD A THICK, broad layer of petroleum jelly
or mentholated rub around tree trunks or stems
of plants being "farmed" by ants.

STOP INVADERS

PROTECT CARROT CROPS from rust flies and
other infestations by hilling the soil around
them, as with potatoes, or sprinkling wood ashes
or coffee grounds onto the soil when you plant
the seeds. Some gardeners have success against
rabbits with the old-time practice of poking
matchsticks into the soil near each carrot.

Mosquito Madness

To launch a counterattack
against mosquitoes, set a
large fan on the porch or
deck where you'll be
eating, and crank it up to
high. Mosquitoes stay out
of windy areas.

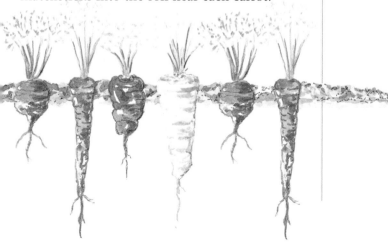

Fool the Birds

Drape and twist narrow strips of silvery, lightweight Mylar through the branches of fruit trees and tie long streamers of it to the branches. The flashing light, which resembles fire, frightens and confuses birds.

Use a scarecrow, and include something—wind chimes, prisms, and kitchen utensils—that makes noise or flashes or moves in the wind.

Paint big, scary eyes onto a helium-filled Mylar balloon, and tie it to a fence or tree to frighten the birds from crops and fruit. Move the balloon every few days to keep the birds guessing.

Discourage birds from feasting on raspberries, currants, and gooseberries by entwining the bushes in thick, black thread.

Victorians tied up their currant and gooseberry bushes with rope. Bunch up the gooseberry branches with twine or strips of cotton (or the legs of panty hose) so it resembles a tightly gathered bouquet tied in three places, and the berries will be hidden in the foliage. This works best for young bushes.

Researchers at Cornell University found they could reduce fruit crop damage from birds by 50 percent by spraying plants with a solution of sugar water. Dissolve 11 (yes, 11!) pounds of sugar in 1 gallon warm water and spray the bushes.

To deter crows from sampling corn seedlings: pound stakes randomly around your corn patch, then thread string between posts and across the patch. The string will look like a giant spiderweb.

To stop birds from eating or pecking fruit, drape dark-colored polyester netting (you can buy cheap stuff in 6-foot widths) over fruit trees or bushes. Attach netting with clothespins.

Dissuade crows from raiding newly planted beds by laying sheets of aviary or chicken wire loosely over the ground. The slightly undulating surface confuses them.

Mole Medicine

To repel moles, mix
the following ingredients:

    8 tablespoons

    castor oil

    1 gallon water

    1 tablespoon liquid

    soap

Dig down into one of the
critter's runs, and pour
the mixture inside.
They'll find digs
elsewhere.
   Try dropping some
crushed cloves of garlic
into the run, too.

WIND TUNNELS

TO DISCOURAGE MOLES, sink a line of glass bottles into the soil with about 1 inch of neck exposed. The weird whistling sound of wind blowing across the bottle tops disrupts moles' sensitive hearing and hinders their ability to find prey.

🐾 Disturb moles' peace by poking noisy little toy windmills into the soil throughout your yard. The vibrations will drive them away.

GOPHER IT

🐾 Keep gophers in their place and out of yours by stuffing ammonia-soaked rags into their tunnels.

🐾 Plant living barriers of oleanders and gopher purge around areas to be protected.

🐾 Create raised beds, and line the bottoms with hardware cloth (heavy-gauge wire mesh sold in hardware stores).

🐾 Protect special plantings with ½-inch mesh fencing 2 feet below the ground and 2 feet above.

MICE-CAPADES

TRY THESE MANEUVERS to keep mice away from your plants:

🦋 Make collars out of hardware cloth or steel wool to protect tree trunks from nibbling mice (stops rabbits, too).

🦋 For small trees, cut the top and bottom off a 1-gallon plastic jug, slit the side to fit the jug around the trunk, then close it with duct tape.

🦋 Sprinkle garlic powder around trees, plants, and bulbs. Reapply after a rain.

🦋 Spray the exterior foundation of your potting shed with white vinegar or ammonia.

🦋 Stuff entry holes with stainless steel or copper scouring pads (not steel wool, as it rusts), and caulk or putty over the pad.

Take a Powder

To keep carpenter ants from harming wooden structures, surround porches and garden buildings, with a band of diatomaceous earth or silica aerogels.

Spray into hard-to-reach areas with a narrow-tipped plastic squeeze bottle. Repowder the area after a rain.

Caution: Always wear eye and nose protection when applying.

The Buck Stops Here

MOST GARDENERS AGREE that a strong, tall fence (preferably electric), tilted at a 45-degree angle, or two fences about 5 feet apart, are the longest-lasting solutions to a deer problem. But, in case a fence isn't in your budget, or doesn't fit in with your garden design plans, here are some alternatives:

Use cloches to protect your plants and get an earlier harvest.

Protect small plants with cloches made from plastic milk jugs, bottomless bottles, screens, or floating row covers—thin sheets of material that let light penetrate but keep out bugs, birds, and animals. (They can be found at any garden center.) Prop the row cover up on chopsticks, cover the tips with grated-cheese shakers, and weigh it all down with rocks.

Dangle strips of Mylar from branches. The constant flickering and flashing alarm deer.

Drape rosebushes and other favorite shrubs under thin sheets of dark polyester netting (it's nearly invisible), and secure with clothespins.

For small garden plots, or to protect some favorite bushes, spread chicken wire on the ground, and allow it to undulate. Afraid of catching their hooves in the wire, deer will avoid the area.

String fishing line around small garden plots at about 2 feet and 4 feet high. Or string the line in a weblike pattern through the bushes on the perimeter of your garden. Deer can't see the line, and once they bump into it, they avoid the area.

Many seasoned deer battlers swear that dirty undies hung on bushes will keep deer far away. My only suggestion is, do this at night, and try to remember to remove them before your neighbors wake up.

Soap Hang-up

Poke a hole with a needle and fishing line through tiny hotel soap bars (wrappers on, and the smellier the better) and hang several on each bush or tree. The Smithsonian's Research Team found Lifebuoy soap to be the best deer deterrent.

Going offensive with dirty undies

Spread dog and human hair clippings (the dirtier the better) on and around plants, or stuff the hair into mesh bags and hang them throughout the foliage. I tried this with clean hair, and it had no effect, but after two days of not shampooing, it did the trick. While you're at it, spread a little urine, too—human, dog, coyote, fox—all but the human kind are available via catalog.

THREE STINKING SAUCES

Rotten eggs and beef bouillon are ingredients in many commercial deer repellents. Break a dozen eggs into a bucket, add 4 cubes of beef bouillon, and fill with water. Cover with a lid and let sit until the mixture stinks. Add 2 tablespoons liquid soap per gallon of water, hold your nose, and spray the plants.

PLANTS DEER DON'T LIKE

Here are the plants that deer usually don't touch, but remember, when deer are hungry, ANYTHING's fair game.

acanthus
agapanthus
ageratum
aster
astilbe
bachelor's
  buttons

barberry
bay
bee-balm
bottlebrush
boxwood

buddleia
calendula
California poppy
Canterbury bell
columbine
coreopsis
cosmos
crocus

The longer rotten egg sauce sits, the stinkier it gets.

Spray plants with Coast of Maine Fermented Salmon, its odor is worse than the most fetid pair of tennis shoes. Many Maine islanders, whose gardens are seriously threatened by deer, swear that this treatment lasts up to 4 weeks. **Caution:** Don't do this before an outdoor party or picnic; it will drive your guests indoors (or away).

Spray with Garlic Soup (recipe page 32) or try Hinder, a commercial repellent made from ammonium soaps, that can be used even on edible plants.

day lily	jasmine		tansy
dicentra	juniper	penstemon	trumpet vine
euphorbia	lantana	salvias	veronica
ferns	lavatera	scabiosa	violet
foxglove	mahonia		wintergreen
geranium			wisteria
holly			
iris			

RUNNING OFF RACCOONS

RACCOONS CAN CAUSE havoc in your gardens and containers. These two methods of deterrence are endorsed by The Humane Society of the United States:

🦋 Sprinkle garlic powder, cayenne pepper, black pepper, or Tabasco on the soil around treasured bulbs or other plants, and the raccoons will keep their distance.

🦋 Run a single strand of low-voltage electric wire around the area you want to protect. The wire need be only a few inches (6, at most) off the ground. I did this around my pond, where the raccoons were raiding nightly, and they never returned. My wire is on a light sensor and comes on only at night, when raccoons are out hunting.

OUTSMART THE COLORADO POTATO BEETLE

🦋 Never plant potatoes in the same plot two years in a row. Beetles overwinter in the soil, and will attack potatoes when they emerge. Cover plants with a mulch of straw or kelp, or use floating row covers.

🦋 Plant potatoes in a bottomless half-barrel or bushel basket and hill as you would in your garden. When the basket is full, surround the potatoes with repellent onion and garlic plants—a successful combo that's been used for centuries against the potato beetle.

SLUGS AND SNAILS, A GARDENER'S TRAVAILS

🦋 Collect cut hair from local barber shops and sprinkle it on top of the soil. A full shoe box covers 100 square feet.

🦋 Scatter pine needles, coffee grounds, crushed eggshells, or diatomaceous earth to provide a scratchy barrier around plants you want to protect. Reapply after a rain.

🦋 Copper strips produce a shock when snails and slugs try to cross them. Purchase inexpensive, thin copper in craft stores, and wrap pots, plants, and trees with a protective band. (Many gardeners lay these strips perpendicular to the ground for good contact with the antennae.)

🦋 Use long strips of metal screen, about 5 inches wide, and bury them 3 inches down into the soil. Copper screen can do double duty: the jagged top stops invaders from crossing.

Spot Treatment

Use long-handled cooking tongs to pick up slugs and drop them into hot, soapy water.

MIRACLE MUD

SOIL SCIENTIST Dr. Michael Glenn and entomologist Dr. Garp Puterka developed the kaolin spray, which changes a plant's surface and not only makes it unrecognizable and inhospitable to insects, but also increases photosynthesis and protects it from sun scald.

Stop injurious codling moths from attacking your developing apple trees and laying eggs on tree trunks with a weekly regimen of a kaolin clay mixture called Surround At Home (see Resources, page 189). Begin spraying as soon as petals drop from the blossoms. The rough, gritty powder acts as an impenetrable barrier for both egg laying and feeding. Repeat weekly for 8 weeks.

Kaolin spray zaps codling moths and cucumber beetles.

Surround® At Home

Halt cucumber beetles, codling moths, and leaf-hoppers in their tiny tracks with a barrier of Surround At Home. Check your journal or calendar (see page 4) and spray plants before the beetles arrive in your garden. These innocent-looking beetles and their larvae, the corn rootworm, are responsible for damage to sixty-one types of crops and innumerable garden plants.

WASPS TO THE RESCUE

TRICHOGRAMMA WASPS, which you can order from certain garden supply centers (see Resources, pages 189–90), will attack codling moth eggs on your apple trees.

These wasps fit through the eye of a darning needle.

THE COVER-UP

COVER BEDS OF PLANTS such as lettuce, brassicas, asparagus, and small plots of corn, which are constantly attacked by insects, with floating row covers or fine netting. If the insects can't reach the food, they can't do any damage. (These covers also discourage rabbits, mice, and deer.)

MR. McGREGOR'S CURES

🐛 Lay down small branches of spiny holly leaves as a barrier around plants to protect them from rabbits and other ground-feeding critters.

🐛 Encircle plants being eaten by rabbits (or snails) with the large, dried, prickly seed vessels of the liquidambar (sweet gum) tree. Gather the pods in the fall, and store in a dry area. In early spring, place them firmly in the soil surrounding the plants.

🦋 Shake baby powder on young seedlings.

🦋 Sprinkle garlic powder on plants.

🦋 Many organic gardeners surround prized bushes with a thick planting of garlic and wormwood, which they claim offends rabbits' discriminating sense of smell.

WAYFARING WOODCHUCKS

🦋 Whenever you cut your hair, or your dog's hair, scatter it along the edges of your garden beds, and woodchucks will veer off course.

🦋 To thwart an invasion of woodchucks, drizzle pure vanilla extract (no cheap stuff for these connoisseurs) onto nice lettuce in a Havahart trap. The furry garden pirates can't withstand the temptation.

🦋 Install a short, L-shaped, chicken-wire fence around beds plagued by hungry woodchucks. The leg of the "L" should trail along the ground about 1 foot (facing away from the garden).

ALUMINUM FOILS

PLANT PATHOLOGISTS in Mississippi found that if you spread aluminum foil on the soil around tomatoes, peppers, and squash, you can prevent viruses transmitted by thrips and aphids. Basil also flourishes with this protection and the extra warmth and light.

🦋 Tape aluminum foil to the fences or walls behind tomatoes and peppers to increase light and heat and to discourage and confuse insects.

🦋 To deter cutworms and stop tomato blight, wrap tomato stems in a sleeve of aluminum foil (buried at least 1 inch into the soil). Use the same technique with squash and cucumber vines to halt borers in their tracks.

AROMATIC ARMORY

PROTECT PLANTS that are often attacked by pests with an antifeedant spray composed of fragrant essential oils. Available in health-food stores and herb shops, oils of peppermint, corn or Japanese mint, and pennyroyal have antimicrobial, insecticidal, and repellent properties.

Mix ⅛ teaspoon (10 drops) essential oil and ⅛ teaspoon liquid soap in 1 quart water. Spray on the foliage of beleaguered plants. Use caution when mixing; pure essential oils are highly concentrated extracts composed mostly of volatile fatty acids, and may irritate the skin.

Gardenside First Aid

If you're bitten or stung, press a crushed garlic clove or slice of onion directly onto the insect bite. Leave on at least twenty minutes. These kitchen favorites have antiinflammatory, counterirritant, and antibacterial properties.

...L O V E J O Y'S B E S T T I P S...

Saucers of water

are the easiest way

to lure good bugs to the garden

(and hope that they stay).

5

Using Lures
TO ATTRACT ALLIES

W
e all know about the bad bugs in the garden, but there
are also good bugs and other helpful critters that you'll
want to lure into your yard. An unseen (or overlooked)
workforce is out there just waiting to get an invita-
tion to help in the garden. If you're like
me, you can use all the allies you can
get to defeat the critters destroying your
plants. First, you'll need to keep your
environment poison-free. Then, to keep
everybody happy, it takes food (a diverse
array of plants), water, and an assortment
of simple and seductive lures.

For the Birds

Birds can rid your garden of many unwanted pests. To attract numerous species of birds and promote a healthy, well-balanced garden, choose the seed-producing plants birds love:

black-eyed Susans

coneflowers

coreopsis

cosmos

feverfew

millet

scabiosa

sunflower

Allow a dead tree stump to remain standing if it's not a threat to you or your home. Dead trees house, feed, and encourage insect-eating birds such as chickadees, wrens, flickers, nuthatches, and woodpeckers to stay in your garden. They also provide homes for rodent-eating predators such as owls, hawks, and kites.

In orchards and vineyards, lure rodent-eating hawks and owls onto the grounds by placing "T" posts at least 10 feet tall, every 100 feet.

Birds Welcome

Encourage insect-eating birds to set up house by furnishing them with nesting materials.

Stuff a mesh bag with narrow grasses, fine strips of bark, thistle, milkweed, feathers (many birds prefer white feathers), or cattail down. Hang the bag in a sheltered area protected from rain and cats.

Feed the birds and foil your foes by placing a board in a shaded, moist area of your garden. Slugs and bugs seek shelter beneath such a hideout. Turn the board over each morning and allow the birds to pick it clean for you.

Set up a platform feeding station (or sunflower seed feeder) to attract chickadees, nuthatches, finches, or other birds that will pluck hundreds of loopers and cabbage worms from your garden daily.

Water attracts birds through every season, even in the worst winter storms. Put out birdbaths, shallow saucers of water, or a fountain with a trickle of water.

Berry-bearing shrubs and fruit trees attract thrushes and other insect-eating birds. Here are some to choose from:

barberry
blueberries
coffeeberry
cotoneaster
crabapples
cranberries
currants
dogwood
elderberry
grapes
holly
mahonia
pyracantha
roses
serviceberry

BAT EXPERIENCE

WHILE BATS AREN'T the prettiest critters, they're some of the best pollinators, seed dispersers, and pest fighters in the world. On warm nights many bats eat nearly their body weight in insects, so it's worthwhile to attract them.

Little Brown Bat eats on the wing.

Illuminate a portion of your yard with a mercury-vapor lamp or incandescent lights. Moths and other garden pests flock to the light; bats will quickly follow, and feed.

Install a set of old shutters to attract and house bachelor bats. Mount the shutters at least 15 feet high, on the sunny side of a barn, garage, or outbuilding. Bats like to slip through the narrow slats and hang from them.

Place bat houses (see Appendix, page 181) on 10- to 15-foot-tall posts throughout your garden.

BORAGE BENEFITS

APHID LIONS (the name says it all), the offspring of green lacewings, are one

Lacewing

of your best allies against all sorts of pests. Recent studies in Switzerland have shown that more eggs and young of the lacewings are found among borage than anywhere else in the garden. If you interplant borage among your vegetable and flower crops, you will eliminate many pest problems.

Aphid lion

SLOW BUT SURE WINS THE DAY

BOX TURTLES feast on slugs, snails, insects, and grubs. They're slow but thorough garden patrollers and great helpers.

LEAP OF FAITH

PROVIDE A TROUGH, half-barrel, or small pond to welcome frogs. They consume slugs, grubs, insects and larvae, and other invertebrates. Refrain from applying herbicides, pesticides, and chemical fertilizers near water.

ROCK HOMES

INVITE INSECT-EATING TOADS, box turtles, salamanders, and lizards into your garden by placing small piles of wood or rocks in secluded areas of your yard. (See Appendix, page 182, for how to construct a permanent wood pile.)

When "Toad" Meant Respect

"In such favor do toads stand with English market gardeners that they readily command a shilling apiece . . . and as toads possess no bad habits, every owner of a garden should treat him with the utmost hospitality."

—British newspaper, 1890

Alligator
Lizard

Heart-wise

The Native American Cahuillas sing an Uska lullaby that calls the dragonflies from the sky. They believe that dragonflies will only land on the pure of heart.

TOAD ABODE

SET A POT half buried on its side in a shady area among plants troubled by loopers, earwigs, and slugs.

Or, chip a toad-sized hole along the rim for a door, and set a pot upside down in your garden. Apply a thick layer of mulch to the surrounding ground for a hideout and supply of insects.

DEBRIS DEPOSIT

SMALL PILES of leaves or needles throughout your garden attract predatory ground beetles. They feed on insects, grubs, slugs, and snails.

Beneficial ground beetle

Jerusalem crickets feast only on dead and decaying vegetation. They're seldom seen because they do most of their good work at night.

INSECT PATROL

FIREFLY LARVAE, the luminous glowworms found in gardens, are voracious eaters, with an appetite for larvae, mites, slugs, snails, and cutworms.

Entice them into your garden by leaving some ground unmowed, or plant some native grasses and wildflowers, and refrain from spraying pesticides. The glowworms will thank you by gobbling up your problems.

DRAGONFLY LURES

DRAGONFLIES can consume 300 insects a day. Lure them to your yard with an old tub, trough, or small pool filled with water. Stick tall bamboo stakes into submerged, soil-filled pots, making sure the twigs protrude above the water. Dragonflies like to perch on these stakes.

Multicolored darner

LADYBIRD SYRUP

LADYBIRD BEETLES and their young larvae, aphid wolves, feed on aphids, scale, whitefly, mealy bugs, and mites. Attract them by mixing 5 ounces

Aphid wolf

sugar in 1 quart water. Shake well and pour into a spray bottle. Spray onto aphid or scale-infested plants, but don't spray directly onto the beetles; it will cement their wings together.

Loves of the Ladybird

Sunflowers, cosmos, dill, anise, fennel, alyssum, daisies, and coreopsis provide the nectar and pollen ladybird beetles love.

The Good Guys

ON COLD, EARLY-SPRING days, when many plants and fruit trees are in bloom and imported honeybees are still snoozing, our native pollinators the bumblebees, orchard mason bees, and flower flies are out and about, ensuring bountiful crops for our gardens and orchards.

Salt, minerals, nectar, and moisture are necessities for butterflies, skippers, and bees. In a sunny area out of the wind, set out shallow saucers containing moist soil and a sprinkling of salt.

Place a flat rock in the soil, drop a dab of jelly or a moist cube of sugar on top, and watch the butterflies zoom in to sip the sweet juice.

Or take the one-step approach: set saucers with rotting fruit throughout your yard.

Lure native bees to your garden with a grouping of wooden bee homes (see Appendix, pages 181–82).

Stuff old coffee cans with lengths of slender bamboo shoots, sunflower stalks, and elderberry canes, and mount the cans in a sheltered location, for example, under a roof.

Mason bee apartments

Beneficial insects and butterflies need small, accessible supplies of sipping water. Grow cup plant (*Silphium perfoliatum*), which has a tiny, water-catching basin at the base of each leaf.

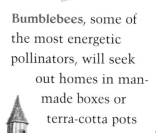

Bumblebees, some of the most energetic pollinators, will seek out homes in man-made boxes or terra-cotta pots

(see Appendix, pages 181–82). Drill ⅝-inch holes to allow bumbles in and to keep mice out.

Butterflies will seek shelter inside a leaf-filled can. Nestle coffee cans filled with leaves and pine needles in the crotches of trees, or nail them to fences and walls protected from the prevailing winds.

Sphinx moth

A hedge of bountiful, blooming four o'clocks will attract sphinx moths to your yard. These lightning-swift insects can pollinate more than two hundred flowers in less than seven minutes.

Sphinx moth

Horning In on Moths

That frightening-looking worm eating your tomato plant is the hornworm, the caterpillar of the sphinx moth. To watch the hornworms do their work, you'll have to sacrifice one tomato plant. Cover the plant with cheese-cloth and close the tent with a clothespin. You'll be the midwife for the sphinx moth, one of the best pollinators in the world.

Hornworm

Snakes Alive!

In Acoma Pueblo, the oldest continuously inhabited village in North America, Native Americans set bullsnakes (constrictors) free in pantries and homes to get rid of rodents.

FOR GOODNESS' SNAKE

SNAKES HELP CONTROL small rodents and many insect pests, and 99 percent of snakes found in yards are harmless. (There are only a few poisonous species in the entire United States; consult a good reptile book to learn if there are any in your area.)

🦋 If you have a rock wall, insert a plastic drain pipe horizontally into the rocks at ground level and leave the pipe slightly exposed to provide access for reptiles.

🦋 Make a space for snakes. Mound some twigs and branches, cover them with a black tarp, and weight the edges with rocks. (You can disguise the mound with a layer of mulch.)

Reading back through a journal is like visiting old friends.

MIGHTY MITE

ATTRACT PREDATORY MITES with potently scented wintergreen. Soak some cotton balls in pure oil of wintergreen. Stuff the balls into empty ½-ounce vials, wrap the necks of the vials in nooses of wire, and hang them wherever mites are a problem. Predatory mites will be attracted and stay to consume pests and their eggs.

🦋 To fight bad mites, mix a solution of 1 tablespoon pure oil of wintergreen (found in health-food stores) and 1 tablespoon liquid soap in 1 gallon water and spray infested plants.

EIGHT-LEGGED PEST BUSTERS

GARDENERS ARE JUST NOW realizing what Chinese farmers have known for millennia—that a garden or field filled with a diverse population of spiders promises rich productivity. Spiders are responsible for about 80 percent of the biological control in a healthy garden.

🦋 Turn terra-cotta pots upside down (holes up) in your garden. Spiders enter the holes and take up residence. They'll tackle earwigs, sowbugs, and beetles, and feast on larvae emerging from the soil and heading toward the light.

"Did you ever think how a bit of land shows the character of the owner?"

—Laura Ingalls Wilder

Green lynx spider

"It is by studying little things that we attain the great art of having as little misery and as much happiness as possible."

—Samuel Johnson

🦋 Furnish spiders with a recycled home made from an old produce crate, and turn it upside down in borders, beds, and fields. Soybean growers who have experimented with crates in the midst of their fields found that pest damage to plants was less in the immediate area surrounding the spider boxes.

🦋 Build small twig mounds throughout your garden to shelter spiders, or stack a permanent rock-pile home for them.

🦋 Mulch your beds with grass clippings and compost; this supplies spiders with a dark, moist, sheltered environment from which to launch bug patrols.

🦋 Always avoid using broad-spectrum pesticides, which destroy spiders and a host of other beneficial insects.

Three small spider apartments

WORMS OF ENDEARMENT

WORMS WORK MAGIC as they eat their way through the earth, leaving behind a vast network of slime-sided tunnels and rich mounds of nutritious castings (worm manure). Their excavations improve soil structure, increase aeration and root penetration, and allow water to percolate slowly and deeply into the ground. Before you mulch your beds to encourage a worm population, the most important thing is to stop using harsh fertilizers and pesticides.

Look Before You Squish!

Greenish, maggoty-looking larvae could be the beneficial and hungry young syrphid or flowerflies, which consume dozens of aphids each day. Most important, they're out early in the season and are on the job before the ladybird beetles.

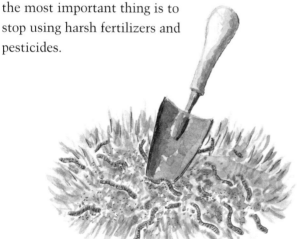

Larva of flowerfly feasting on aphid

...LOVEJOY'S BEST TIPS...

Although the act of thinning

is a nasty little chore,

For every seedling weeded,

you'll end up with much more.

Great Expectations

STARTING WITH SEEDS

"When first the soil receives the fruitful seed
make no delay, but cover it with speed!"

—Virgil, *The Georgics*

I remember the first time I planted a seed, and my wonder (mixed with disbelief) that such a small, flat, dry-looking capsule could contain the makings of a plump, orange pumpkin. To this day, I am filled with childlike excitement whenever I hold seeds in the palm of my hand and contemplate the miracle inside each one.

The smaller seeds
plant shallow,
The bigger seeds
plant deeper.
If you forget this
simple rule,
Your seeds will all
be sleepers!

Nothing gives you more value for your money than a packet of seeds. Spend some time browsing seed selections in catalogs (see Resources, pages 190–91), and you will discover an array of plants seldom found in nurseries. For just a few dollars, you will be able to plant rare heirloom varieties once cherished by your ancestors, wildflowers from your childhood, or a diverse selection of vegetables with tastes unrivaled by market produce.

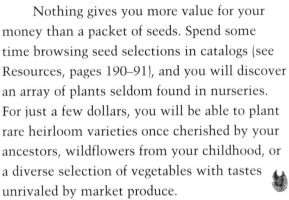

You won't find a litany of basic how-to-plant directions in this chapter; that subject is well covered in many books. Instead, I want to share some shortcuts and oddball planting tips that always work well for me.

RULE OF GREEN THUMB

SEED COVER (the soil atop seeds) is one of the most important keys to success. Bury seeds to a maximum of three times their diameter, and be sure to keep them moist or the germination process will stop. The tiniest seeds need only be shaken across soil and patted into place. A gentle watering with a fine spray secures them.

RUBDOWN

SCARIFY IMPERMEABLE seed coats (such as lupine and morning glory) by rubbing them across a small piece of drywall sanding screen (100 grit). Staple the screen near the edge of your potting bench, place the seeds on the screen, and rub them back and forth with a block of wood. If you don't want to wrestle with a sanding screen, brew a cup of hot tea and drop your seeds into the water for an overnight soak.

My child's-eye view of seed coats

IN THE BEGINNING

GERMINATE LARGE SEEDS (such as moon vine, morning glory, or gourd) between two sheets of damp paper towels. Wet the towels thoroughly, sprinkle the seeds across one sheet, top with another, and tuck the wet towels into a clear plastic bag. Check the seedlings in a week. If you have green sprouts, it's time to plant them in soilless potting mix. Sow the seedlings in a 1½- to 2-inch-deep tray, or in homemade paper pots filled with moist potting mix. Water them gently and enclose the tray or pot in a plastic bag or plastic wrap— you're creating a mini-greenhouse. Then set the plants in a warm, well-lit area.

Scarifying Plants

Camellias, ceanothus, dogwoods, hawthorns, lupine, manzanita, morning glories, redbuds, sweet peas, tree peonies, and wisteria are some of the most common plants whose seeds need a rubdown.

A Brush with a Feather

Early colonists used turkey feathers to gently brush soil over their tiniest seeds. You can do the same with any large feather, or an artist's soft-bristle paintbrush.

MAGIC PENCIL

USE A PENCIL as a triple-duty tool. End the frustration of trying to perfectly space and plant tiny seeds. Sharpen a lead pencil to a fine point, and dib it into moistened planting mix—it must be moist to work—to the correct depth. Lightly touch the tip of the lead to a seed, and it adheres like magic. Gently poke the seed into the hole. Use the eraser end of the pencil to cover the seed with the planting mix.

TOILET PAPER TAPE

TO HELP KEEP SEEDS spaced well apart, you can buy Paper Planting Tapes—or you can easily make your own seed tapes. Mix some water and flour to a thin consistency and paint it (or squirt it from a squeeze bottle) onto the center of a long piece of toilet paper. Sprinkle fresh seeds into the moist goo. When it's dry, place the tape on a weeded and prepared bed.

Fill an empty grated-cheese container with soil, sprinkle a light dusting on top of the tape, and water thoroughly. Keep seeds moist until germination, then water as needed.

SEED SHAKER

MAKE THE CHORE of sowing tiny seeds easier by mixing them with a handful of fine sand in a grated-cheese shaker. Then, rake your bed or prepare your pot, and shake the seed mix lightly onto the soil.

GROUND COVER

MANY OF THE TINIEST seeds and seedlings are eaten by slugs or birds. However, for some reason birds won't touch a bed that's covered with small chipped gravel, and slugs won't traverse the sharp terrain. When planting, spread a thin layer of gravel across the potting mix or soil, then simply shake the seeds on top and water thoroughly. The gravel acts as a protective mulch and reflects light and heat.

"Nothing which gives us a happy hour can be insignificant."

—Dr. George Johnston, 1858

OUT, DAMP SPOT

PREVENT DAMPING-OFF, a fungal disease that attacks and destroys seedlings, especially those started indoors and in greenhouses. If your seedlings are wilted, have keeled over, or have a rotten spot at the base of their stems, there's a good chance they have this fungus. Remove any sick plants and toss them into the trash.

Now use a damping-off fork "rake" to cultivate the soil around the remaining plants. Provide plenty of light and good air circulation (try a small fan set on low), and water seedlings with chamomile tea (see page 33).

PICK A POT

FILL THE CONTAINERS described here with soilless seed-starting mix, drop in the seeds, and water thoroughly.

FRUIT POTS

EMPTY RINDS OF grapefruits, lemons, limes, and oranges make excellent little starter pots. You can transplant rinds directly into the garden soil.

THE ECO-WAY

THOSE PLEATED PAPER drinking cups you find at the water cooler make great expandable little

pots. Place the open end of the cup against your mouth, and give a strong blow; the cup will expand to more than double its size. When you're ready to transplant, just slit the sides of the cup and place it in the garden.

Or make your own biodegradable pots. Using a soup can as a mold, wrap two sheets of newspaper around the outside of the can, fold the leftover paper to shape the bottom, and tape it to hold it in place. Run a piece of tape around the center to strengthen the sides, then slip the paper pot off the can. Recycle empty milk cartons, soupcans, Styrofoam cups, yogurt and cottage cheese containers, and take-out food containers as planters. Make sure to provide drainage holes.

Egg-citing Start

Cardboard egg cartons can be recycled into perfect seed-starting flats. When it's time to plant, separate the sections with a sharp knife, and tuck each one into the soil. The cardboard will decompose as the seedlings grow.

Back Saver

Sometimes the mere
thought of bending over
one more bed or border to
plant seeds is unbearable.
To cut down on bending,
use a 4-foot length of
narrow pipe as a dibber,
drop the seed down the
pipe, and cover with soil.

RADISH MARKERS

HELP YOUR TINY SEEDS push their way through
crusty soil by planting "markers"—larger,
tougher, faster germinating seeds—nearby.
Victorians always planted the round, robust
seeds of radish along with their tiny carrot seeds.
Markers not only break the crust for the smaller
seeds, but also delineate exactly where they're
planted—a great aid when you're weeding.
Use radish marker's for your poppies, evening
primrose, and other tiny seeds.

WARM PAD

IF YOU'RE STARTING seeds indoors in a cold
cellar or porch, you might want to draft your
heating pad into service (it must be suitable for
moist heat). Many plants need soil that's at least
50 degrees to germinate. So warm it up with a
pad set at the lowest setting.

HOMEMADE PAD

PROFESSIONAL GROWERS reduce their irrigation chores and keep plants moist by setting containers on capillary mats—fiber pads that hold moisture and keep it moving. Make your own mats by laying a sheet of black plastic on the ground and topping it with 10 to 12 sheets of newspaper. Place your potted plants on the newspaper and water them thoroughly. Runoff is absorbed by the paper, then slowly released back to the plant. (You can use these mats for about 2 months; then throw them into your worm bin or compost pile.)

GREENHOUSE ON WHEELS

A STATION WAGON or van (with windows) can double as a temporary greenhouse and protect your seeds and seedlings from birds, squirrels, and insects. Lower the rear seats and spread plastic across the bed. Move newly sown flats and pots onto the plastic, park your car in a partially shaded location (cars heat up rapidly), and roll the windows down a few inches. Water as needed.

> "Into the prison of the seed comes water, the liberator!".
>
> —D. C. Peattie

True Leaves

When the halves of the opened seed coat remain attached to the stem, they resemble leaves. True leaves are the first set of actual leaves, and resemble those of the parent plant.

CHOPSTICK TENT

POKE CHOPSTICKS into a newly prepared and seeded bed. Place small plastic bottles over the exposed ends of the chopsticks (so as not to rip the material). Cover the bed with a sheet of floating row cover or coarse cheesecloth. Hold the edges down with small rocks. Water with a gentle spray. The cloth protects seeds from washout, slugs, snails, and seed-eating birds. Remove the cover when the seedlings show two sets of true leaves (see sidebar).

HAIR TODAY, GONE TOMORROW

BURY PIECES OF human or dog hair around seedlings to deter the critters who try to feast on them. Hair also contains nutrients that will nourish young seedlings.

THIN IS IN

OVEREXUBERANT SOWING of seeds leads to a thick mob of seedlings, and if they aren't thinned, none of them will thrive. Because pulling out seedlings can injure the survivors, use cuticle clippers or small scissors to cut the extras at soil level.

FAVORITE PICK

IF YOU WANT TO save the seeds of your favorite annuals and perennials, tie a colorful ribbon on the stems in bloom. After the seeds have flowered, find the ribbon, enclose the seed head in a brown paper bag, and tie it closed. Clip the stem and hang the bag indoors to dry. Remember to label the bag with the flower's name and description.

GRANDMOTHER'S METHOD OF SEED STORAGE

1. Clean and thoroughly dry (this is imperative) old plastic or glass jars and lids.

2. Take a stack of four unfolded facial tissues. Into the center of the tissues, scoop 2 tablespoons of powdered milk from a newly opened container.

3. Fold the tissues over the powdered milk into a flat packet and tape the packet closed.

4. Pour the seeds you want to store into a clean envelope, label with the date and the seed variety, and seal the flap.

5. Tuck the pouch of powdered milk and the envelope into a covered jar. Keep the jar closed. Replace the milk packet with a fresh one after 6 months.

6. Store the container in the refrigerator to keep the seeds cold and dry.

7. For storing seeds, the colder the better. Each 10-degree drop in temperature means you double their longevity.

...LOVEJOY'S BEST TIPS...

Here's a fact

there's no getting 'round:

a bare patch of earth isn't

good for the ground.

Chapter Seven

THE GENIUS OF
The Ground

T his may sound corny, but I love my soil. I'm so proud of the dark, rich texture, and the way the water soaks slowly out of sight and into the ground. But it wasn't always so. When I first moved to Seekhaven, my old California cottage, two decades ago, the earth had large bare patches that were as hard as rock, baked by the sun, and eroded by water runoff.

Mulch, compost, and worm castings (manure) deserve all the credit for how it looks today. A constant regimen of adding these ingredients to the top layer of the ground—I never disturb the structure of the

> "And let no idle spot
> of earth be found,
> but cultivate the
> genius of the ground."
>
> —Virgil, *The Georgics*

soil with unnecessary tilling—is your single most important task. It is literally the groundwork for a healthy and bountiful garden.

For cultivation and propagation practices, I often turn to the long-forgotten tried and true techniques of the early settlers and the Victorians. Willow water, potato cradles, and milk-fed pumpkins are just a few of the whimsical but successful pointers I divulge here.

WILLOW WATER

SCIENTISTS AND RESEARCHERS recently confirmed something herbalists and gardeners have known for centuries. The tender spring tips and leaves of willows, the easiest of all woods to root, contain powerful hormones that stimulate the growth and development of plants. No need to buy chemically produced rooting compounds when Mother Nature has a supply as near as a willow tree.

Collect tender twigs and leaves (the highest concentration of rhizocaline compounds are in the protoplasm of the newest growth), cut them into 1-inch pieces, and drop a few fat handfuls into a bucket. Fill the bucket with water and steep the mixture for a week.

Strain and decant the tea-colored liquid into small canning jars. Store in the refrigerator. (Jars of willow water make great gifts for gardeners.)

For a quicker fix, bring 1 gallon of water to a boil, and turn off the heat. Drop the willow into the pot, cover, and let the mixture steep overnight. Strain and decant into small containers. Keep them refrigerated.

When propagating plants, dip the fresh cuttings into willow water, let them soak for a few minutes, dib a hole into your potting soil, tuck in the cutting, pat soil firmly into place, and water thoroughly with the willow water solution.

POTATO CRADLE

FOR PROPAGATING finicky shrubs, nothing works like this tried and true secret first written about in the 1850s. Cut a slip of your plant on the diagonal. Tuck the cutting immediately into a hole in a small potato—you're creating a potato cradle! Prepare the ground or a container for planting, add compost, set the potato into

Potato moistens, protects, and feeds a cutting.

the soil, and cover it completely, leaving only the cutting above the surface. Water gently, and tend as you would any newly propagated plant. This is a nearly foolproof method to start stubborn, woody plants.

Dark Beginnings

Dr. Makota Kawase of the Ohio Agricultural Research and Development Center discovered that fresh rose cuttings root faster if they're kept in total darkness for the first 4 or 5 days. I like to stick my potted cuttings into a brown paper bag along with a ripening apple. The ethylene gas from the apple speeds up the process.

GREEN GLASS FOR ROSEMARY

FAMED HORTICULTURIST Gertrude Foster's unique method for getting finicky rosemary cuttings to root was to start them in green glass bottles filled with water. It still works for me every time. Rosemary will begin to show roots within a few weeks and you can transfer the cuttings to a pot of soil.

PROPAGATING ROSES

IF YOU HAVE TROUBLE propagating roses, use the old 3-4 formula first touted in the early 1900s.

Take a 4-inch cutting just above a node with at least 3 sets of leaves. Stick the stem into willow water for 1 hour. Then dib a hole in a pot of moist sand and stick the rose stem into the hole. Cover tightly with a mini-greenhouse (plastic bag or wrap, or bottomless plastic bottle).

It may take a couple of months for the first roots to form, but once they do, you can transplant the rose into freshly dug soil enriched with compost (see the banana peel hint on the next page).

BANANA PEELS FOR ROSES

SOAK BARE ROOT roses in a bucket of willow water overnight. Dig a hole in a sunny area, and build an elevated mound of compost in the center. Set the rose atop the mound, spread the roots out gently, snip a banana peel (high in potassium, phosphorous, and magnesium) into tiny pieces, and drop them into the hole. Cover with humus and soil, tamp firmly, then soak the ground thoroughly.

WINTER WRAP FOR ROSES

TO PROTECT a prized rosebush from the ravages of winter and frost heaving, surround it with a cylinder (taller than the canes) made of box wire or chicken wire. After the ground freezes, top the canes with a mound of loose soil and fill the entire cylinder with straw or leaves. Cover the cylinder with a large plastic bag tied tightly to the frame. Remove the bag when spring growth resumes, clear the soil from the canes, and spread the leaves around the rose for mulch. Give the rose a thorough soaking with Container Champagne (page 26) or organic fertilizer.

"The rose looks fair, but fairer it we deem For that sweet odour which doth in it live."

—Shakespeare

A Rose Is Not a Rose . . .

If you want old-fashioned roses with a heavenly fragrance, you need to find heirloom plants. Check out the specialty suppliers under Resources, page 190.

ROOF ROSES, NANTUCKET STYLE

ROSES LOVE and require sunshine, and sometimes the best sunlight is on the roof. I was inspired by the cottages on Nantucket Island, where I saw my first rose-festooned roofs in the historic village of Siasconset.

Make lift-up boxed frames with two-by-fours set on end. Attach a trellis to the top of each frame and latch frames to the roof with heavy-duty hooks and eyes. Keep your constructions in easy-to-handle sizes appropriate for the roof area.

The boxed frame allows for plenty of ventilation, and the trellis lifts easily for trimming or repairs. In summer, the roof will be cloaked in colorful, fragrant roses; in fall and winter, the glowing globes of rose hips add a dash of brilliance (and food for the birds).

Rose hips add a fall touch of color

SKIP THE SALT

🦋 Stop the habit of using rock salt to de-ice walkways and drives. As snow melts, the salt filters down into the soil, injures roots, and can kill plants. Instead, use complete NPK (nitrogen, phosphorus, potassium) garden fertilizer to de-ice anything that's near landscaping. Spread the fertilizer in the same quantities recommended for salt. The potassium, or potash, will melt the ice, and the phosphorus will provide a slip-proof surface.

🦋 Stash sand in a covered container near frequently walked pathways, and use a coffee can or scoop to spread it.

🦋 Apply 10 pounds of urea per 100 square feet of pavement to melt ice, and add a sprinkling of sand for traction.

🦋 Use a small propane torch, such as the ones used on weeds, to quickly de-ice walkways. (See "Burn the Bad Guys," page 40.)

"The real voyage of discovery consists not in seeking new landscapes, but in having new eyes."

—Marcel Proust

VICTORIAN ROT PREVENTION

TO PREVENT cuttings from rotting, spread a 1-inch layer of clean sand on top of potting mix. Use a pencil as a dibber, let some of the sand trickle into the hole, insert a cutting, and pat the soil firmly around the stem.

GROWING A PRIZE-WINNING PUMPKIN

MAKE A THRONE for your pumpkins. Curl a piece of box wire into a cylinder, fasten the ends together, and stand it upright. Fill the wire enclosure to the brim with grass clippings, leaves (preferably shredded), vegetable refuse from the kitchen (and the water you cooked the veggies in), shredded newspaper, and shredded garden debris interspersed with layers of soil. Tuck in pumpkin seeds, and cover with compost. Your pampered pumpkins, treated like royalty on their rich throne, will flourish and their vines will quickly disguise the wire. Championship pumpkins will be yours if you cull the small ones until only the biggest and

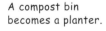

A compost bin becomes a planter.

healthiest remain on the vine. Water, feed them regularly, and treat them to a gallon of whole milk every other week.

AN UNCOMMON GREEN

CULTIVATE WATERCRESS, an old-fashioned favorite that adds zing and a peppery taste to sandwiches and salads. Purchase a plant from a nursery (or gather in the wild and set in clear water for a few weeks to purify the plant) and fill a pot (this is one time you don't want a drainage hole) with soil mixed with sand. Drench your soil with willow water mixture or clear water.

Gently separate the stems (each one will eventually sprout), dib a hole into the wet soil with a pencil, and plant the cress about 3 inches apart. Set the pot in a partially shaded area and keep the soil soggy. Within a few weeks, you'll be able to harvest these greens for salads. Use the cut-and-come-again method and snip only the outer leaves each time you harvest them.

Bumper Crop

Protect vulnerable shrubs and trees from weed-whacker or lawnmower accidents. Keep a plastic bottle (slit down the side with the top and bottom removed) tied to your machine. Stop before working too close to plants and slip the bottle around the trunk while you weed or mow in that area. Remove the bottle when you move on.

HELP FROM KELP

FOR CENTURIES, seaside gardeners have valued and used seaweed as a garden mulch and food. For a healthy, no-work potato patch, dig a hole about 1 foot deep and as long as you want your patch to be, and fill it to the brim with seaweed. Plant your sprouted seed potatoes, cover them with a 6- to 8-inch-high mound of seaweed, and forget about them until harvest time.

POTATO COUCH

SPROUT YOUR seed potatoes in an egg carton. Set the potatoes rose end (fattest end) up. This end produces the best sprouts.

FOOL THE CLEMATIS

CLEMATIS ARE FUSSY about where they grow; they prefer to have their heads in the sun and their feet in cool shade. If you don't have the required shade, you can fool the vine by simply placing broad, flat stones at the base of the plant.

SETTING THINGS STRAIGHT

HERE'S A FOOLPROOF way to keep a line of trees or plants perfectly spaced.

Cut notches into a long board at 1-foot intervals. When you need to plant trees, shrubs, or perennials with specific space requirements, lay the board on the ground and align the plants with the notches.

PROPAGATE FINICKY LAVENDER

SOMETIMES IT'S IMPOSSIBLE to grow a hedge of
lavender of uniform height, but there's an
old-time method of uniformly propagating this
fragrant shrub that's simple and easy.

Give your favorite lavender a crew cut. Using
hedge shears, cut the top foliage of a lavender bush
flat. Then dig up the plant—root ball and all. Split
the root ball into vertical pieces, with the old
wood and foliage still attached.

Plant the lavender pieces in well-
drained soil at least 3 feet apart (unless
you're planting the tiny Hidcote or
Munstead varieties). Spread a layer of
light-colored pebbles, sand, or chipped
granite beneath the plants to reflect
light and deter soil-borne diseases.

FAN IT OUT

WHEN BEARDED IRIS stop producing flowers after 3 or 4 years in the
same area, gently dig out the rhizomes,
and save the biggest with the healthiest
leaves. Use a sharp knife to separate
the clumps, trim the roots, and cut
leaves to about 6 inches. Allow the

"A good day's
work can be
done with a
dirty spade."

—Old saying

"Ere yet the planter undertakes his toil,

Let him examine well his clime and soil;

Patient explore what best with both will suit,

And, rich in leaves, luxuriantly shoot."

—Richard Payne Knight

clumps to "rest" overnight before planting. Space the rhizomes about 18 inches apart and barely cover the roots with soil (don't bury the fan of leaves). Water thoroughly. Properly planted iris looks like a family of green-tailed swans sailing across the garden.

MINT CONDITION

OLD PATCHES OF MINT often turn into tangles of roots and stems with few or no healthy, flowering stalks. Each spring, score the mint patch checkerboard style, about 1 inch into the soil, with a sharp knife, and new growth will quickly emerge from each small square.

Tennesseans, famous for their mint juleps, have a tradition of presenting a new bride with a gift of mint plants dug from the family garden.

MUCH ABOUT MULCH

MULCH, MULCH, and more mulch. Through every season (even in the worst winter weather), mulch's macro- and microscopic armies are at work in your garden. Mulched soil is high in ethylene gas, which discourages the growth of fungus and other pathogens (from the Greek *pathos,* meaning disease). Microbes in composted pine and hardwood barks enhance microbial activity and suppress diseases and root rot.

Mulched earth supports unseen billions of beneficial underground dwellers that enrich the soil and improve its structure. Soil protected by a layer of mulch also retains moisture, prevents soil-borne diseases from splashing up and onto plants, deters invasive weeds, prevents erosion, and provides a welcoming environment for spiders, ground beetles, and other helpful garden critters.

MULCH WITH THE TIMES

THE NEW YORK TIMES, that is, or any newspaper. For garden pathways, spread a thick layer (about 30 sheets) of newspaper, then top the paper with 3 inches of shredded bark.

For beds, apply a thick layer of *damp* newspapers, leaving narrow spaces for row crops. To plant individual perennials or bushes, cut into the damp paper and tuck the plants into the soil. Top the beds with finely shredded bark, leaves, or grass clippings.

Chop, Chop

Save your leaves, and put
them through a shredder
or run your lawnmower
through piled-up leaves to
shred them. Or dump the
leaves into a trash can
and use a weed whacker
to shred them. Top your

beds with the
shredded leaves,
and don't
worry, they won't
change your soil pH.

LET IT SNOW, LET IT SNOW

MULCH WHEN soil is freezing. You can even
apply mulch on top of snow. As the snow melts,
the mulch settles onto the soil
and releases nutrients.

CLOSE ENCOUNTERS

LOOK LOCALLY for abundant sources of mulch—
wheat, leaves, grass clippings, soybeans, cocoa
hulls, shredded corn cobs, kelp, mussel, and
clam shells . . . you get the picture.

ORGANIC METHOD

MANY GARDENERS and farmers have stopped
using strips of black plastic for mulching
because plastic is costly and isn't biodegradable.
A new alternative is brown kraft paper coated
with boiled linseed oil.

Even more inexpensive and equally healthy
is to buy wrapping paper by the roll, coat it with
canola oil, and allow it to air-dry. Cut the sheets
to fit your beds.

For a new bed, spread the paper in the garden and top it with shredded bark, grass clippings, or straw. Poke holes through the mulch
and paper to plant seeds or seedlings. By the end

of the growing season, the paper will already be decomposing and becoming a part of the earth.

BY THE BAG

SEE IF neighbors will give you their bags of leaves in the fall. Store the bags out of the way in your yard and ignore them. Within a few months you'll have some fine, rich compost to spread throughout your garden.

A HEALTHY DOUGHNUT

CREATE A BIG doughnut of mulch, then plant your trees and shrubs in the center. Take care to keep the trunk at least 6 inches from the mound to prevent rot and rodent damage. Replenish the mulch doughnut 3 to 4 times a year.

COMPOST HAPPENS

NITRO BOOST

ACTIVATE YOUR COMPOST pile by adding alfalfa meal, Litter Green kitty litter, pelletized rabbit food, or dry dog food, which is rich in nitrogen and protein. Nitrogen-rich green grass clippings (without chemicals) will also help.

The Stripper

Keep the branches of small, fragile conifers from breaking under winter ice or snow. Use 2-inch-wide strips of fabric. Tie one end to the base of the tree and spiral-wrap up to the top, then back to the base, to secure the branches.

"Of composts shall
the Muse descend
to sing."

—John Grainger, 1770

JUMP-START YOUR COMPOST

PROVIDE NEW COMPOST piles with a large scoop of finished compost from your old pile. The hungry microbes from the old compost will stimulate the new, sluggish pile and speed up the process of decomposition.

WORM PETS

EVEN APARTMENT dwellers can compost with red wiggler worms, the world's most undemanding pets. These hungry invertebrates have an appetite for garbage and will quietly transform your leftovers (and culinary disasters) into castings, known as "black gold."

Use the castings to top the soil of houseplants, as well as outdoor containers and garden beds. Once you share your life with worms, you'll wonder how you ever got along without them.

You can purchase a worm bin kit or make your own for indoors or outdoors (see Appendix, pages 183–85). Worms are content indoors if kept warm (55 to 77 degrees), fed, and watered regularly. They must always be kept moist.

WILLOW WILL GROW

WHEN YOU CUT a willow branch and plant it in damp ground, it will immediately strike roots and sprout. Use this magical quality of the willow and plant a living willow screen to hide an unsightly compost pile. Cut fresh willow rods about 4 feet long. Dig a narrow trench 12 inches deep around the area you wish to hide and fill it with good aged compost. Stick a line of rods, about 8 inches apart, a few inches deep into the trench at a 45-degree angle, then lay another line the same distance apart in the opposite direction, making a crisscross pattern. At each end of the screen, sink a wooden or metal pole about 2 feet into the ground to strengthen the structure. Cluster at least 5 rods around the pole and tie them loosely together.

> "The highest reward for man's toil is not what he gets for it, but what he becomes by it."
>
> —John Ruskin

OUT-OF-SIGHT COMPOST

DON'T THROW AWAY that holey old plastic trash can; reuse it as a fast-acting composter. Remove the bottom of the can with a box cutter or snips. Drill about 2 dozen 1-inch holes into the sides. Cut a sleeve of scrap screen to slip down into the sides of the can (the sleeve should cover all the holes).

Dig a hole at least 2 to 3 feet deep and the same diameter as the can. Set the can in the hole and fill in the sides of the hole with mulch, leaves, straw or hay. Add alternating layers of wet and dry material and mix with a pitchfork every two weeks.

MY GRANDPARENTS' COMPOSTING PIT

COMPOSTING DOESN'T NEED to be a fancy or laborious process if you use the method of my grandparents (and thousands of other gardeners). Dig a hole at least 3 feet square, and toss your garbage, grass clippings (high in nitrogen), leaves and straw (high in carbon), shredded wet newspaper, and kitchen waste (not meat or dairy products) directly into the hole. After each addition of garbage, just add a layer of soil, leaves, grass clippings, or a mixture, and cover the hole with a screen, weighted down along the edges with a board framework or rocks. The screen excludes flies and predators, but allows rain to trickle into the hole.

If you plan to plant a tree next spring, a compost hole is a great way to prepare the soil for it. Just plant your tree directly into the hole once it's filled with compost, and it will have all the nutrients it needs.

TRENCH COMPOSTING

DIG A LONG, shallow trench at least 2 feet wide and 2 feet deep in an unused area of your garden. Work your way down the trench, daily dumping garbage, clippings, and leaves into it. Cover the refuse with soil and a board to exclude critters.

Compost ingredients: everything but the kitchen sink

Never let weed

set seed.

Chapter

8

Lawn & Weed

FOUR-LETTER WORDS FOR WORK

"A lawn is nature under totalitarian rule."

—Michael Pollan, *Second Nature*

Y ou're ahead of the game if you plant a lawn with disease-resistant cultivars that are proven successes in your area. Check with your local nurseryman, co-operative extension, or Master Gardeners for the varieties best suited to your area. Lawns should be for picnics, croquet, and a game of touch football, not for backbreaking labor.

WATERING GUIDE

POKE A RAIN GAUGE into the lawn to check the amount of water it receives. One inch of water should soak to a depth of 4 to 12 inches, depending on the composition of the soil. Test the depth of water penetration with a moisture monitor and aim for a 6- to 8-inch soaking each week to develop longer, healthier roots and grass.

Water your lawn and garden early in the morning to reduce evaporation.

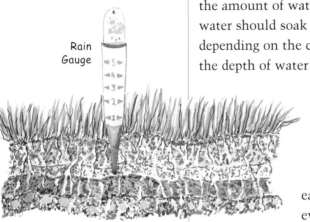

Rain Gauge

"Home would not be home without a lawn."

—Katherine S. White

TENDING

THINK ORGANIC. Feed the soil, not the grass. Mulch your lawn with grass clippings (which return nitrogen to the turf), shredded leaves, and compost.

Test the soil pH before adding any fertilizer (See Resources, page 189). Add only the nutrients the soil needs, then fertilize in the spring and fall. Fall feeding is the most important. It builds up food reserves so grass is stronger and greens up faster in the spring.

MOWING TIPS

🦋 Use a mulching mower to cut the grass into small pieces and spit the clippings back onto the lawn. You never have to rake, and the clippings feed the lawn.

🦋 University of Wisconsin Research Stations advise keeping your lawn 3 to 3½ inches high, perhaps an inch longer during high heat. The height of the blades is equal to the depth of the roots, and deeply rooted grass is more drought tolerant.

🦋 Wipe or spray a mower blade after each mowing with a 10 percent solution of alcohol to prevent the spread of pathogens.

🦋 Sharpen mower blades regularly to prevent tearing of the grass, which weakens it and invites disease and pests.

🦋 In the fall adjust the mower blades for a lower cut, which will reduce disease problems caused by long, moisture-trapping grass blades.

🦋 Hurrah! You can stop mowing when grass growth slows or stops in late autumn.

🦋 Always rake leaves off grass to prevent matting and disease.

Tread Carefully

Chickens, ducks, geese, and wild birds love to feast on your lawn's enemies, but beware of going bare-foot after they've worked the territory.

LAWN PESTS

GRUBS AND BEETLES

LAWNS are often plagued by a number of pests, but the most common and destructive are sod webworms, cutworms, grubs of Japanese beetles, and armyworms. In early summer, you may notice brown patches of dead turf or small, grayish moths flying low over the grass as they deposit eggs. These are sure signs of an unwelcome invasion of pests.

These invaders thrive in stressed, compacted lawns with a thick thatch and large, sunny, dry areas. One of the best strategies for fighting the invaders is to water deeply and only as needed (in contrast to daily shallow sprinkling). Other remedies include using a dethatching rake to remove the thick covering, and dancing across the lawn in aerator sandals

Dethatching rake

Good mite

(this reduces Japanese beetle grubs by over 50 percent), or using a hand or power aerator (see Resources, page 189) and feeding the lawn with compost or grass clippings. Robber flies, wasps, mites, beetles, and beneficial nematodes (see Resources, pages 189–90) prey on these pests, too.

Beneficial beetle

Use a shop vacuum to remove pests from the lawn. Dispose of them in hot, soapy water.

WEED WRANGLING

A WEED IS ANY PLANT you didn't intend to grow. There are thousands of plants that could be considered weeds, but the general rules for getting rid of any unwanted plant are the same.

Walk your gardens each morning (you'll be surprised what you can accomplish in just a few minutes) and check any disturbed ground, such as the edges of borders and walkways and newly prepared beds. Weed seeds will quickly gain a foothold in exposed and disturbed areas. Pull or hoe any young weeds immediately.

"One is tempted to say that the most human plants, after all, are the weeds. How they cling to man and follow him around the world, and spring up wherever he sets his feet!"

—John Burroughs, 1890

Stirrup hoe (far left) and colinear hoe for weeds.

 ## Gardenside First Aid

Get acquainted with plantain, a ubiquitous weed found almost everywhere. You can mash the leaf and apply it to a fresh wound. Hold the leaf in place with a clean bandage or wrapping. Plantain contains allantoin, an antiinflammatory compound that heals injured cells. It can also be used to draw out splinters.

Weeds thrive in disturbed ground, and will grow in any bare soil. Mulch exposed soil with grass clippings, shredded leaves, pine needles, newspapers, compost, or bagged, shredded cedar or bark chips.

Invest in a few recycled rubber soaker hoses to prevent weeds, and cut down on soil-borne diseases caused by the splatter of mud and water. These thick hoses never flail about the garden as lighter-grade hoses sometimes do. They'll deliver more water directly to the plants (not weeds) that need it, and you won't lose valuable water to evaporation.

Dislodge young weed seedlings when they first appear with a hula, colinear, or stirrup hoe. Just drag the hoe across the top inch of the soil. For deep-rooted weeds, use a forked-tongue tool (called a daisy grubber) appropriate for the size of the plant. Dispose of weeds in an active (over 140 degrees) compost pile or in a trash can.

🐞 Pull or dig larger roots (such as dandelions) by hand, and make sure you get out all of the root. If you simply hoe dandelions, the deep root will resprout.

🐞 Zap young dandelions, thistles, and other broad-leafed weeds with a directed stream of household vinegar (5 percent acidity) and a few drops liquid soap for coverage (this is a spot solution, and not for wide areas). Apply in the heat of the day.

🐞 Mow or weed-whack right after weeds flower, but before they set seed. If you let them go to seed, you'll have successive generations of hardy survivors.

OUTSIDE THE BOX

USE THAT LITTLE BUTANE kitchen torch you normally reserve for crème brûlée (these tiny torches are best for tight spaces such as cracks in pavement or rock walls), or purchase a back-pack flamer that has a propane torch specifically designed for weed control. Flame the weeds early in the spring when they're just emerging. There's no need to sizzle them; just slowly pass the flame about 1 inch above the plant, and the cell sap will heat up and cause the cell walls to burst. Within a day, your weeds should be dead.

> "The utmost attention is necessary never to suffer weeds to perfect their seeds in any part."
>
> Bernard McMahon, 1806

🦋 Pour boiling water directly onto the weeds. This works especially well when they're firmly settled into cracks in sidewalks, stonewalks, or flagstone patio. (Don't do this to poison oak or poison ivy.)

🦋 Plant a cover crop of clover or buckwheat to smother weeds and enrich the soil.

🦋 Spread a thick layer of newspaper (about 30 sheets) on the soil and cover it with straw, bark, shredded leaves or compost.

RENT-A-GOOSE

SAVE YOURSELF HOURS of backbreaking labor by enlisting the aid of a goose, one of the best weeders in the backyard labor force. These fowl love narrow-bladed weeds and will uproot them from dawn to dusk (and bright nights) seven days a week.

Weeder geese (as they are known) are safer than hoes, which can damage roots, and they give you a value-added bonus with their fertilizer. The University of Tennessee Agricultural Experiment Station recommends geese as a perfect chemical-free method of weed control and fertilization.

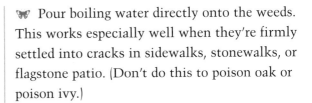

CORN GLUTEN MEAL

PROFESSOR NICK CHRISTIANS and other researchers at Iowa State University found an amazing use for corn gluten meal—the tough, sticky, elastic by-product of milled corn meal. The protein-rich corn gluten meal contains an herbicide that suppresses weeds, crabgrass, and dandelions by inhibiting root formation during germination. And the effect lasts for months!

To protect a newly planted (but not seeded) bed from a weedy invasion, work corn gluten meal into the top 2 to 3 inches of your soil, and water thoroughly. Don't fertilize the bed for a month after application because corn gluten meal is high in nitrogen.

Timing is everything; if the seeds have already germinated and sprouted, this won't be effective. Top-dress your lawn and flower beds with nitrogen-rich corn gluten meal.

Drag a sharp putty knife across small plants or weeds poking through cracks in pavement or asphalt, and sprinkle corn gluten meal into the cracks to prevent further seeding.

Gardenside First Aid

In case of contact with poison oak or poison ivy, use soap and hot water immediately to wash the affected area, but don't take a hot bath or shower. If you don't have access to soap and water, put mud on the affected area and scrub vigorously. Repeat the process several times, using fresh mud. Pat fresh mud onto the surface of your skin and let it dry.

ABOLISH POISON OAK AND POISON IVY

LEASE (OR BORROW) A GOAT

GOATS ARE THE BEST destroyers of poison oak and poison ivy, and they can climb in terrain where machinery can't reach. Fence off any trees, bushes, and plants where you don't want the goats, then let 'em at it. Goats are browsers and would rather eat brush than grass. They strip bark from shrubs, eat twigs, and reduce fire hazards by chomping their way through overgrown weeds.

Goats don't heed
the warning: leaflets
three, let it be.

IF YOU PASS ON THE GOAT . . .

When ridding your yard of poison oak or poison ivy, always wear long-sleeved shirts, gloves, socks, long pants (tied or rubber-banded to prevent branches from poking inside), and boots or high-topped shoes.

Many persistent gardeners cut these plants back to the ground as soon as the first new leaves appear. This weakens the roots and eventually kills the plant.

Using a hand sprayer, douse the leaves with a solution of isopropyl rubbing alcohol, white vinegar, or real alcohol. My husband once dumped all the leftover drinks from a cocktail party into a bucket and used it to destroy a whole patch of poison oak.

After the leaves drop off in the fall, expose the poison oak or ivy roots with a long-handled hoe, and pour boiling water onto them. Try to keep the steam away from skin and clothing. Then cover the roots with a sheet of clear plastic to solarize and destroy them.

Caution: Never pour boiling water on the leaves of the plant. You can get an allergic reaction from the oils in the steam.

Gardenside First Aid

If you aren't near water or mud, rub freshly crushed jewelweed on the area exposed to poison oak or poison ivy. This must be applied ASAP. Jewelweed contains lawsone, an active ingredient that quickly blocks out urushiol, the oil that causes the rash. The highest concentration of lawsone is in jewelweed's knobby, reddish roots near ground level.

"Give me the splendid, silent sun, With all his beams full dazzling."

—Walt Whitman

HARNESSING THE SUN

IF YOU HAVE an area that's impossible to keep clear of weeds and invasive grasses, let the hot summer sun (temperatures above 85 degrees) work for you in a process called "solarization."

Water the area deeply and regularly for 2 weeks, which will give weed seeds time to sprout. Rake away any plant debris and cover the *wet* soil with clear 4-mil plastic (UV-resistant, if possible). Make sure the plastic contacts the soil. Tuck the edges firmly into the ground, or weight the edges with rocks or boards. Let the bed "cook" for 4 to 6 weeks, then remove the plastic. Scientists have found that solarized soil kills many harmful nematodes and microorganisms, but doesn't harm beneficial nematodes and microorganisms.

Apply corn gluten meal (see page 127), water thoroughly, and top the bed with a thick layer of mulch, newspaper, or grass clippings.

WEED-FREE SOLUTIONS

Attack broad-leafed weeds with a directed stream of vinegar. You may substitute vinegar with equal parts water and isopropyl alcohol

(70 percent solution), but be careful not to spray any treasured plants. This works well for areas in stone or brick patios where you don't want grass or weeds. Drench the leaves with liquid. Cover nearby plants with newspaper to protect them from overspray.

Lay down pieces of cardboard and top them with shredded bark (at least a 3-inch layer), then let the bed "rest" for a season. Next spring, the cardboard will be like mulch, and the bed will be weed-free and easy to work.

Sun Speak

When seed packets and plant labels direct you to situate your plants in "full sun," that means they need at least 6 hours of full summer sun a day. The most intense light of the day is between 10 A.M. and 2 P.M.

For outdoor decor

you don't need a lot.

Just look at your garden

and use what you've got.

Chapter

Outdoor Decor

The urge to decorate every inch of my environment (the proverbial nesting instinct) is still with me when I venture out into the garden. No matter where I work, I always try to create small vignettes, focal points, enticing vistas, and intimate seating areas for conversations, meals, and just plain relaxing.

I discovered long ago that sometimes the simplest container, tool, or rock stands out as beautifully in a landscape as a fancy, high-priced piece of garden sculpture. Now I experiment and try to create ephemeral arrangements of found, natural materials, such as leaves and flowers, or carefully considered clusters of pots, tools, and handmade willow-work trellises, *tuteurs*, and tepees.

Go outside today and find a small spot that needs a face-lift. Then look at what's at hand with fresh eyes and an adventuresome spirit. You'll be both surprised and satisfied with what you create for your garden. Happy nesting!

TROMPE L'OEIL FENCES

SEARCH FOR OLD multi-paned windows to mount on uninteresting walls or expanses of fence. You can leave the windows unadorned or paint a scene behind the glass and add shutters and a window box.

Attach an iron or wooden gate or door to a solid wall or fence at the end of an axis line or pathway. The portico will become a beckoning focal point and hint at secret places beyond the boundaries of your garden.

BORDERLINE

TO CREATE A whimsical border, parade a matched line of small terra-cotta pots along your flower bed.

OUTSIDER ART

CREATE YARD ART from cast-offs. Extricate those old tools from your garage, and use heavy-gauge wire to fasten them together into a three-dimensional sculpture or a gardener's coat-of-arms. Mount them on large L-shaped brackets screwed into a fence or wall. Or bunch the tools together, tie them loosely, and allow them to stand on their own as vertical assemblages in the garden.

Terra-cotta Repair

To repair a broken terra-cotta pot, moisten the breaks, squeeze carpenter's glue onto the broken edges, and reset the pieces. Circle the pot with strips of masking tape to hold the pieces in place, and let the bond harden.

FLOATING BOUQUETS

TURN A BIRDBATH into a work of ephemeral art. Float an array of blossoms and fronds on the water when you expect company or you're hosting an outside celebration. I did this in our toilets, and it was a big hit with guests, until they wanted to flush!

LEAF A TRAIL

GATHER FRESHLY FALLEN leaves or flowers and arrange them in whimsical designs on garden pathways and terraces.

SHEDDING LIGHT

🐾 Outfit a terra-cotta pot with an electrical wire and socket, and use it as a hanging lamp for a potting shed, garden room, porch, or greenhouse.

🐾 Pick up some old wire-handled canning jars at flea markets or antique shops and give them new life as outdoor lights. Pour 1 inch of sand or gravel into each jar, nestle a candle in the center, and hang them along porches and tree limbs or parade them up a drive or pathway.

🐾 If you have a crop of hard-shelled gourds, you can create your own lighting fixtures. Pick the gourds after the vines dry and store in a cool, well-ventilated and covered area. Hang-dry the gourds in panty hose or recycled mesh potato or onion bags. They're dry when they feel light and rattle when shaken. Use a saw to remove the narrow top third of the gourd, and drill holes in patterns around the sides. Set a small glass holder and votive candle inside.

🦋 Amass a stash of quart and half-gallon cardboard drink containers to use as molds for magical winter lights. Remove the tops, and slide a quart container into a half-gallon carton. Drop rocks into the quart carton to hold it in place. Pour distilled water between the two cartons. Let freeze. Just before use, pour some warm water in the smaller container and lift out. Peel the outer carton from the ice block. Line a pathway or driveway and drop in tea lights or pillar candles. They'll look like flickering fireflies.

SECOND-HAND PLANTER
PULL THOSE WORN-OUT gardening gloves from the trash can and use them as charming hanging planters on a wall or fence. Make sure there are drainage holes in the fingers, fill the gloves with soil, and plant them with lettuce, radishes, baby carrots, flowers, or small, trailing plants.

Use Hues
Long Island gardener and artist Robert Dash uses color as one of the most important elements in his bold garden designs. He fearlessly paints gates, fences, and furniture to match the season or satisfy a whim.

Marking Your Territory

Snip your own plant labels out of 16-ounce (a thin weight that bends easily) sheets of copper. With an awl, poke a small hole in the end of the copper, and thread it with copper wire. Or cut out a T-shaped marker that can be poked into the soil. Write the names of your plants with a ballpoint pen or a grease pencil.

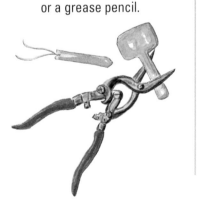

CENTER STAGE

HIGHLIGHT YOUR FAVORITE plants by moving them to center stage on a patio, porch, or frequently visited walkway. Turn two or three terra-cotta pots upside down and lay an old board across them to serve as a staging area.

TOTEM STORAGE

ATTACH A SERIES of three terra-cotta pots horizontally to a tall vertical post in your garden. Keep plant labels, markers, and twine inside. Although these look like totemic garden sculptures, they're practical and will save you lots of steps.

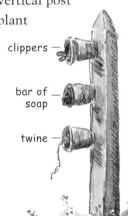

clippers —

bar of — soap

twine —

THE NATURAL LOOK

GATHER LONG BRANCHES or slender tree limbs to build a series of tepee-shaped trellises for your garden. These vertical structures are focal points, punctuation marks in a normally horizontal plane. Grow annual vines on the tepee, with shade-loving lettuces inside. The shade will also stop your lettuces from bolting.

Collect sculptural, twisted lengths of driftwood or windfall branches to construct wall trellises and arbors. Predrill the holes to avoid splitting the wood, then fasten the branches to each other or to a wall with galvanized deck screws.

Turn a coal hod
into a planter.

Display an array of empty
containers for impact.

A bouquet
of tools

Metal Works

Assemble a whimsical collection of old pieces of galvanized metal (chicken feeders and waterers, buckets, coal hods, watering cans, florist's buckets, and so on). The pewter patina is a perfect foil for the colors and foliage of plants. For greater impact, mass the pieces closely together.

SEE SHELLS

SEASIDE GARDENERS, or anyone with access to seafood processing plants, can use the shells of mussels and clams as a design element of a decorative parterre. When crushed, the shells make a handsome and long-lasting surface for pathways.

MIRROR IMAGE

COLLECT OLD MIRRORS (even the grungiest glass looks great outdoors) and hang in dark or shaded areas in your garden to reflect light, create the illusion of more space, and evoke a sense of mystery.

RACK THEM UP

A TRIP TO THE junkyard may turn up some fabulous finds that will give pizzazz to your

Chicken feeder
drawer before and after

A battalion of buckets
for every use

garden. Line an old hay rack with moss and
mount it on a wall. Fill it with soil and nestle
show-stopping specimen plants inside. Or cut
a piece of exterior plywood slightly larger than
the top of the rack, paint or marbleize it, and
mount it against a wall or fence to use as a
demilune garden table.

TERRA-COTTA TABLE

TURN A LARGE terra-cotta pot upside down for an
outdoor table base, and top the pot
with a large, upside-down saucer.
This makes a handsome occasional
table near a bench or a
pedestal for potted
plants. Or turn it right
side up and use as a birdbath.

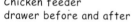

> "What is necessary
> is that we be content
> with little."
>
> —St. Teresa of Ávila

FREEBIES

TERRA-COTTA-COLORED chimney flue and sewer tiles make large, handsome, and versatile planters. These bottomless containers are great for large specimens, such as trees, shrubs, and artichokes. Check out construction sites. Contractors are often glad to give away slightly damaged pieces.

REST IN PIECES

SET 2- TO 4-FOOT sections of chimney flue, terra-cotta sewer pipe, or copper or galvanized pipe 1 foot vertically into the ground. As you move among your beds and borders, rest your unused spades, shovels, hoes, or rakes standing up, with the handle slipped into the pipes.

POST-IT

MOUNT MAILBOXES on walls, fences, and posts throughout your garden. Stow extra work tools, twine, gloves, seed packets, labels, and a small first-aid kit inside. You'll save lots of time and extra steps with these handy mini storage sheds.

STACKED UP

STACK A GRADUATED SET of soil-filled terra-cotta pots to form a tower. Leave a 2- to 3-inch border of soil visible around each level. Plant strawberries in the borders; they'll cascade over the sides.

FRAMED

CUT A "WINDOW" through a hedge and suspend an old multipaned casement window inside to frame a view. To create a circular opening, hang a large willow or grapevine wreath or an oval or round picture frame inside the hedge.

STUMPED

CREATE RUSTIC, outdoor furniture for your kids. Cut a tree trunk into a 2-foot-tall section for a table, and shorter lengths for seats. Sand the tops to prevent splintering.

HANDLE THIS

DRESS UP YOUR garden gates and the potting shed door with handles and pulls made from worn-out trowels, spades, or small digging forks. Protect them with a coat of pure paste wax.

WELCOME SIGN

ADORN YOUR DOOR with a cluster of old gardening hand tools wired together and hung from a hook. Add sprigs of herbs and affix a copper label with a "Welcome" greeting.

THYME CLOCK

TRANSFORM A LARGE, terra-cotta saucer into a living sundial. Drill drainage holes in the bottom, lay screen over the holes to exclude slugs and bugs, and fill the saucer with good potting soil. Plant wedges of different species of thyme.

Use a piece of wood as the sundial gnomon. Cut a right triangle with the angle at the same degree as the latitude where you live—for example, if you live at 40 degrees latitude, make a 40-degree cut. Set the saucer on a raised pedestal or a rock. Position the gnomon so that it runs north-south in the center of the saucer, with the tallest portion aimed at true north,* the twelve o'clock setting. Accurate for telling you when it's lunchtime, and beautiful *all* the time.

*Hint: When the shadow of a vertical rod is at its shortest, it's pointing true north.

ZEN GARDEN

COMPOSE A HANDSOME and simple Zen-like
garden sculpture. Make a shallow wooden box,
fill it with sand, and set a few of your favorite rocks
in place. Use a garden fork to rake a fresh pattern into
the sand every day. Or plant the box (make sure you have drainage holes)
with a ground cover such as fescue, baby's tears, thyme, or blue star creeper,
and nestle a small sculpture or a grouping of handsome rocks into the plants.
The ground cover will carpet the soil, and the rocks or sculpture will look as
though they're growing from the lush green.

GUTTER ART

HOLEY OR DAMAGED metal (especially copper and zinc)
downspouts and gutters make great planters. Mix
trailing specimens along with annuals in the downspouts, and plant small herbs in the gutters. (Remember
to cover the drainage holes with screen.)

HOSE POT

DON'T THROW AWAY that large, rim-chipped
terra-cotta pot; turn it upside-down. To keep
your hose from kinking, wind it around the
base of the pot and stick the nozzle through
the drainage hole.

Indoor
PART TWO
GARDENING

Never water

plants if their soil is wet,

or a fresh crop of fungus

is all that you'll get.

Chapter

10

CONSIDER THE HUMBLE
Houseplant

Dozens of plants crowded the windowsills of my tiny attic apartment in an old Victorian boardinghouse. They were the most companionable and undemanding roommates, and their quiet, green presence was a constant comfort and tonic for me. Tending their simple needs became a reverie, a time of peace and serenity that helped me get through some difficult transitions in my life. I felt that I was part of a large, peaceable family.

Mother Nature's Most Efficient Air Purifiers

Boston fern, weeping fig, Areca palm, rubber plant, and peace lilies top the list of air purifiers.

Many years passed before I learned the scientific reasons why plants make us healthier, although I knew I always felt better when I puttered among them. Health workers now use plants as a therapeutic intervention and rehabilitation tool for people with critical injuries and life-threatening diseases. And after years of research, NASA scientists discovered that the introduction of houseplants will remedy the indoor pollution phenomenon called Sick Building Syndrome, which causes allergic reactions and illness. Just two houseplants for every 100 square feet of indoor space will remove toxins and, through photosynthesis, turn the pollutants into food for the plants and oxygen for us.

Now that you know how beneficial indoor plants are, why spend another minute of your housebound or officebound life plantless? Visit your local nursery or florist, and familiarize yourself with its indoor plant selection. Read the labels to find out plant requirements (don't purchase a light-hungry flowering plant for a dark, basement apartment unless you can furnish it with abundant artificial light), and buy only what you feel you can easily maintain. Caring for houseplants is a gentle labor of love and patience, a matter of getting to know new friends and recognizing how to satisfy their simple but necessary needs.

If you're an advanced gardener, or just adventurous, don't stop with the easy-care plants. Try your green thumb on a few of the more unusual indoor specimens that were popular during Victorian times. Tend a winsome dwarf fruit tree, a flowering hibiscus or camellia, a box of tasty herbs, a window-climbing vine of jasmine, or a troupe of scented pelargoniums.

Take good care of your houseplants, feed and groom them, keep them from temperature extremes, satisfy their lighting needs, don't overwater them (the most common cause of plant fatalities), and your houseplants will take good care of you.

"The best aspect for room plants is the southeast. They seem like animals in their affection for the morning sun."

—*The Gardener's Monthly,* 1871

LET THERE BE LIGHT

IF YOUR HOME is blessed with sunny southern windows, you'll be able to grow everything from flowering maples, orchids, and scented geraniums to voluptuous fruit trees and lofty bays. But, if your conditions are less than perfect, and you're trying to grow plants in a dark northern or eastern exposure, you'll need to supplement your natural lighting with a little help from the electric company.

Some of my best plants grew, thrived, and bloomed

A grow-light can be a simple architect's lamp.

under an old architect's lamp outfitted with a 100-watt bulb. So don't think you have to get fancy or spend lots of money. Gro-lights, fluorescent tubes, and High Intensity Discharge lights are available in hardware and lighting stores and catalogs. If you don't want to fuss with extra lighting or crank up your electric bills, just choose plants suitable for the exposure you have. (See the plants recommended for different exposures in the Appendix, pages 185–86).

SHADY CHARACTERS

I SWEAR THAT some plants will grow just about anywhere—a dark office, lit only by high, overhead fluorescents (and not a window in sight), or a basement apartment that receives just a sliver of sunlight daily. The stalwarts listed here will green up the most inhospitable of spaces. They require almost no maintenance and have low light requirements.

aloe

bamboo palm

bird's nest fern

candelabra cacti

cast iron plant
(the name says it all)

Chinese evergreen

dracaena
(the compact form)

dragon lily

heartleaf philodendron

pathos

peace lily

rubber plant

split-leaf philodendron

tillandsia
(or air plant, which can be hung from curtain rods, picture frames, etc.)

Read Your Plants

Sunburned or bleached leaves, long lanky stems which lean toward the light, and shedding indicate unsuitable lighting. Move pale, sunburned plants to a window with less-intense light. Move lanky, leaf-dropping plants to a brighter area or under artificial lighting, and pinch them back to a more compact form.

Train pathos up a mini-tepee.

Simple Tools for the Indoor Gardener

Keep a selection of spoons, knives, forks, chopsticks (to use as dibbers), and spray bottles handy for small indoor plant projects.

Italian parsley

THE HERBAN GARDENER

HERBS ARE SOME of the most fragrant, tasty, and versatile plants to grow in a sunny southern window or under a Gro-light. Rosemary, oregano, savory, parsley, sage, thyme, mint, and chives will put up with a little benign neglect, and can produce enough trimmings to flavor sauces, teas, and salads. Basil and chervil are a bit more picky, and thrive best during the long, bright days of spring and summer.

Talk to your herbs, turn them weekly for uniform growth, pinch and trim them as needed for cooking, feed them weekly with a half solution of balanced fertilizer, and enjoy every whiff and taste these ancient plants offer.

MOTHER NATURE'S MEDICINE CHEST

NO KITCHEN SHOULD be without a pot of dependable aloe vera, one of the easiest and most useful plants to grow. Aloe will tolerate less than perfect lighting; an eastern or northern window or even a desk lamp will suit it just fine. Start with a small plant, and soon your aloe will produce enough "pups"—their tiny offspring—to fill a pot to overflowing. For burns, cuts, abrasions, or frostbite, slit open an aloe leaf and apply the cool, healing gel.

Aloe vera

EASYGOING SUCCULENTS

SUCCULENTS ARE a forgiving family of plants that will reward indifferent care with healthy growth and blooms of unexpected brilliance.

Echeverias, with their tall, wandlike blossoms, look like waxen sculptures of rosettes. Kalanchoes and Easter and Christmas cacti sport brilliant flowers during the darkest months. Crassulas, mammalarias, and hens-and-chicks provide bold, contrasting textures and forms that stand in stark contrast to the traditional collection of houseplants.

Give your succulents plenty of light, then ignore them. Don't overwater, don't feed, and don't worry.

Echeveria and mammalarias

Water Thief

Always presoak new terra-cotta pots in a sink or bucket of water for 1 hour before planting. Dry clay pots wick the moisture from the soil before the plants can drink their fill.

THE RIGHT STUFF

DON'T USE OUTDOOR garden soil for your indoor plants, or you may introduce unwelcome pests. Buy bagged potting mixture, which you can find at garden centers and an array of stores.

THE WELL-CONTAINED PLANT

CHOOSE FROM a medley of containers for your houseplants—plastic, metal, glazed, concrete, or even an old pair of boots, provided they have drainage holes. Terra-cotta pots look subtle and natural, and they breathe, which cuts down on soggy soil and waterlogged roots, fungus, and mildew. Your terra-cotta containers will require more frequent watering than impermeable materials.

THE ROOT OF THE MATTER

IF YOU NOTICE that water pours down the inside walls of a pot (and the soil shrinks slightly away from the sides) instead of through the soil, or if roots are peeking through the drainage hole, you should slip the plant out and check the condition of the roots. Before removing the plant, follow the directions for a salt soak (page 158), making sure that the soil is thoroughly wet. Examine the root formation. If the root ball is not yet crowded with a network of rootlets, simply clean the pot, add a bit of new soil, and tuck the plant back in place.

If the plant is encircled with a tight wreath of roots or the soil is crowded with roots, it's time for a slightly larger pot. Read on.

SIZE MATTERS

ALWAYS REPOT into a container just one size larger. Small pots usually increase in 1-inch increments; at 10 inches, they jump by 2-inch increments, which will suit your large plants just fine. Repotting into containers too large for your plants will result in a mass of wet soggy soil that can choke or rot plant roots, robbing them of the air exchange they need to survive.

Upgrade only by 1-inch increments.

POTTING UP

WITH THE PLANT out of its pot, use a sharp kitchen knife to make four shallow, vertical slits around the sides of the root ball. This liberates the roots so that they can spread in their new soil. Tease the roots apart slightly, then set the plant in its new container using the method described below.

REPOTTING

COVER DRAINAGE HOLES with small pieces of screen or
pantyhose. Fill the bottom of the pot with a few inches of
moist (not soggy) potting soil. Situate your houseplant in
the center of the pot, and continue to fill it with soil up to
the plant's original soil line. Tamp the soil
gently to remove pockets of air and to firm it
into place. Water and lightly tamp the soil
again so that the level is about ½ to ¾ of an
inch below the rim. You may need to add just a
bit more soil if the level drops. Slowly pour in
water until the pot is filled to the rim, let it drain, then repeat.

Set the pot on a saucer filled with 1 inch of gravel and ½ inch of water.
(You can add activated charcoal, available in pet stores and garden centers, to
clean the water and eliminate the sometimes musty odor of standing water.)

SALT SOAK

WHITE CRUSTING along the rims of your pots indicates a buildup of harmful
salts and residue that can burn a plant. Water the plant, spread your fingers (open
palm) across the top of the soil, turn the plant upside down, and slip it and the
surrounding ball of soil gently from
the container. Soak the pot in a sinkful
of hot water mixed with a cup of
white vinegar. Scrub the salty crust
from the rim with a crumpled
piece of aluminum foil.

FRESH TOPPING

YOU MAY NOTICE that each time you water, some of the soil washes through the drainage holes. When the soil level drops about ½ inch, top it lightly with a fresh layer of potting mixture (usually monthly).

FEEDING

SINCE WATER CONSTANTLY passes through your house-plants' soil, it quickly leaches the nutrients that plants need to live a healthy life. Chemical fertilizers give plants a quick fix, but they can also burn your plant roots, build up salts, and destroy beneficial bacteria in the soil. Many gardeners prefer organic fertilizers derived from ground rock, animal materials, and plant matter.

ORGANIC FERTILIZERS

FEED PLANTS TWICE a month during the active growing season with a balanced organic liquid or a soluble concentrated fish emulsion–kelp blend,

"An indoor jungle is a personal thing. All the rules in the world may be no help. . . . The most important thing is to want to grow the plants."

—Richard Langer

Java Jolt

Save your coffee grounds, and occasionally (about once a month) add a thin layer to the soil of your acid-loving houseplants such as azaleas and camellias.

which contains natural growth hormones (cytokinins), trace elements, and potassium. (See Resources, page 189.) This mixture will build sugars in plants and make them healthier and less prone to disease and insect problems.

GIVE IT A REST

DURING THE WINTER, when plant growth slows, discontinue feeding. Resume feeding again in the spring as your plants begin their growth spurt. But ease into feeding slowly, diluting your normal liquid food by half for the first month.

Note: Before applying any fertilizer, always water your plant thoroughly to prevent the roots from burning. Signs of fertilizer damage include a sudden dropping of leaves and burned spots on the edges of leaves.

SNACKS FOR JAUNDICED PLANTS

WHEN LEAVES TURN yellow from the tips toward the stem—a sign of a serious nitrogen deficiency—treat your plant to a helping of unflavored gelatin. Sprinkle a packet around the base of the plant for a slow-release nitrogen boost. Always allow the soil to dry out between watering.

CALCIUM BOOST

CRUSH CALCIUM-RICH eggshells between two sheets of wax paper and add them to your plant's soil at least once a month. Calcium, a secondary nutrient, encourages the formation of cells and healthy plant and root growth.

GROOMING

JUST AS EVERY head of hair has its own special pattern of swirls, twirls, and cowlicks, every plant has an innate form and posture. We wouldn't dream of going weeks without grooming our hair, and the shaping and grooming needs of plants are just as individually distinct and important.

Begin nipping, cleaning, and pruning plants when they are youngsters. The more attention you pay to their form, the more you'll be repaid with blooms and a well-filled shape. Remove dead or dying foliage, and trim off the growing tip to encourage the full-branching of such plants as azaleas, fuchsias, geranium, and jasmine, or prune back a few inches to just above a node.

Grow new plants from your clippings.

THE WELL-ROUNDED PLANT

PLANTS ARE HELIOTROPIC—they turn and bend toward the sun or artificial light. Make it a weekly ritual to rotate your plants a quarter turn, and pinch the tips of any leggy foliage. You'll be rewarded with lush, well-rounded plants.

THE ELEMENT OF WATER

FINGER TEST

THE NUMBER ONE cause of houseplant fatalities is overwatering. To determine if your plants need water, poke your finger about 1 inch into the soil. If it's dry, water it slowly, and allow the moisture to percolate deeply into the soil. All plants have different requirements, so no preset schedule, no matter how well it works for you, will satisfy their needs.

YELLOW MEANS CAUTION

YELLOW LEAVES and bright green veins, often signs of iron-hungry plants, may also be a warning that you're overwatering. Soggy soils slow or stop the release of iron to plants. Remember to water only when the soil is dry, and use a fork to gently (without harming roots) aerate the soil.

NO WET FEET

TO KEEP YOUR plants healthy and free of fungus and mildew, set them on a tray or glazed saucer filled with about 1 inch of gravel and ½ inch of water. Water early in the morning to carry the plants through the heat of the day, and drain any excess water from the tray (never let your pots sit directly in standing water).

COLD COMFORT

TURN DOWN THE heat and crank up the humidity. Your houseplants are happiest and healthiest when the room temperature is in the 50s and low 60s. During the winter, when furnaces and fireplaces are at full tilt, plants often suffer the ravages of their dry environment. (Look for browning leaves, wilting plants, dropping fronds.) Set pans of water atop radiators and woodstoves, near vents and the furnace, and pull your humidifier out of the cupboard and put it to use.

DRAFT EVASION

BE KIND TO your plants, and rescue them from blasts of icy air from windows, doors, and air conditioners. If the plants are above air conditioners, simply set them on a broad tray or shelf that will deflect the air current. If they're directly in the path of the air conditioner, move them! The same wisdom applies to heat from vents, stoves, and fireplaces. Move your plants out of the immediate area to prevent desiccation and spider mites, which thrive in dryness.

Warm Plunge

If you've forgotten to water a treasured plant, and it's dry, wilted, and looks like it's hopeless, apologize to it, then plunge it into a bucket of warm water (higher than the rim of the pot) and allow it to soak until the bubbles stop rising. Remove it from the water, let it drain, then set it back on a pebble-filled saucer.

SHARE A SHOWER WITH YOUR PLANTS

MOVE OVER AND share the shower with your ferns, rubber plants, palms, and ficus. Give them a warm, gentle spray of water, and allow the soil to become soaked. You'll rid your plants of grease and dust and wash away infestations from mites, mealybugs, and whiteflies. Always shower plants with warm water early in the morning (to prevent fungal diseases), and keep the plants out of direct sunlight until they're dry (or wipe and blot them with a soft cloth or paper towels).

Caution: To prevent mildew, fungus, and spotting, avoid showering hairy-leafed plants (violets, gesneriads, rex begonias) and succulents.

ROLL OUT THE (RAIN) BARREL

PROTECT YOUR houseplants from the harmful effects of hard tap water and fluoride salts (browning leaf tips, injured roots, bound nutrients) by watering them whenever possible with distilled or rain water.

If you do use tap water, treat your plants to a monthly sip of vinegar tea. Mix 1 tablespoon apple cider vinegar in 1 gallon distilled or rain water. Soak plants thoroughly.

Set rain barrels
at downspouts

Fluff Your Ferns

In the early twentieth century, castor oil was considered a tonic for whatever ailed you, but the cure wasn't reserved only for people; it was used on lackluster, droopy parlor ferns, too.

1 tablespoon castor oil

1 tablespoon liquid
soap

1 gallon warm water

Mix thoroughly and drench the soil. Let soil drain, and reapply.

FISHY SITUATION

STINKY AQUARIUM water is filled with luscious nutrients and trace elements for your plants. Whenever you clean your aquarium, pour the old water into a bucket or watering can, and use it on the plants.

VEGETABLE BROTH

EAT YOUR VEGETABLES, but save the cooking water. Let the liquid cool, then water your plants with the broth; it's fortified with trace elements and minerals.

THE TEA CEREMONY

ADD LEFTOVER TEA (or used tea bags) to your watering can. Chamomile tea is antibacterial and fungicidal and will aid plants suffering from fungus and mildew. Use this tea as a foliar spray and on tender seedlings to prevent damping-off. Sprinkle black or green leftover tea on acid-loving indoor plants such as azaleas, gardenias, and camellias.

Share your tea with your green friends.

ENEMA BAG
FOR HANGING PLANTS

ENLIST THE AID of an enema bag
and attachment for those hard-to-
reach hanging baskets and overhead
watering chores. Fill the bag with
warm water and 1 teaspoon liquid
fertilizer. Attach the hose, insert
the tip into the soil, and squeeze
the bag gently and slowly. The water
will infiltrate the soil, and you'll be spared
the annoyance of wet sleeves or of
lugging heavy plants to and from a watering place.

Note: If your hanging plant is suspended from a hook, you can slip the
bag over the hook (there's always a hole at the top) and leave the enema tip
in the soil (about 1 inch).

PESTS

UNWELCOME PESTS are seldom a problem for indoor gardeners who water and
feed as needed, protect their plants from temperature extremes, and provide
adequate light and humidity.

Inspect every new plant for signs of disease *before* you buy it. Look for
mold on the soil surface, signs of plant distress (yellow or browned leaves),
and infestations of mealybugs, whiteflies, aphids, or scale. Pick up the plant

shake it lightly to check for emerging gnat flies. The last thing you want is to introduce disease into your healthy household plants.

If your plants *do* fall prey to pests, turn to these homemade, nontoxic cures. The use of chemicals is more dangerous to your health than a few insects.

BASTER BLASTER

ATTACK COTTONY mealybugs, aphids, and whiteflies, all common enemies of houseplants, with this concoction. Use a baster to squirt directly onto the pests.

    1 TABLESPOON LIQUID SOAP

    1 TABLESPOON LIQUID SEAWEED OR KELP

    1 GALLON WARM WATER

Thoroughly mix the ingredients, fill the baster, and baste away (check the undersides of leaves, too). Wipe off excess moisture with a soft cloth. (Remember *not* to use the baster for your next turkey dinner!)

GNAT MAGNET

TINY, FLYLIKE gnats emerging from your soil are an indication that you have injurious larvae attacking the plant roots. Lure the gnats into a small bowl filled with ½ water and ½ apple cider vinegar. Set the bowl near your plant, and stand back. The gnats (and fruit flies) will line up on the rim and dive in, never to emerge. Empty the contents of the bowl every 3 or 4 days, and refill.

SCALE

WOODY-STEMMED plants, such as citrus and ficus, are likely candidates for scale, a small pest that clings to stems and leaves and sucks the plants' juices. Look for soft, pale yellow blobs (young) and hard, waxy brown bumps (adults) that resemble little turtles. Some species of scale will respond to treatment with a simple spray of insecticidal soap. Here's my homemade version:

> **1 TEASPOON MURPHY'S OIL SOAP**
> **1/2 CUP ISOPROPYL RUBBING ALCOHOL**
> **1 QUART WATER**

Mix thoroughly and pour into a spray bottle. Apply out of direct sunlight. Do not use this spray on plants with hairy leaves.

If the infestation is small, spot-treat scale with a cotton swab dipped in 70 percent isopropyl rubbing alcohol. The scale should lift off the plant with a single swipe.

Loving Up Your Plants

Talk to your houseplants. Touch and shake them gently. Stanford University molecular biologists have discovered that five plant genes are activated when plants are touched. These genes make the plants sturdier and stockier than untouched specimens.

Citrus plants thrive indoors for decades.

A Squirt in Time . . .

To prevent cross-contamination, be sure to squirt isopropyl alcohol onto scissors, knives, or clippers after use on a sick plant. Dispose of dead or diseased foliage.

BUG OFF

SUCK PESTS OFF YOUR plants and out of the air with a small, hand-held vacuum or a canister vacuum with a tube attachment. Hold the vacuum about 1 inch away from the leaves and pass it back and forth quickly above the pests. Empty the contents of the vacuum into a bucket of hot, soapy water.

BUG BRACELET

MAKE A CIRCLE of narrow adhesive tape, sticky side out, around your fingers. Blot the plants, and the bugs lift off.

GOOD USE FOR A BAD GIFT

PUT THAT GIFT of cheap cologne to good use. Lightly mist any visible mealybugs, whiteflies, or aphids. You'll be surprised at how quickly the cologne knocks out pests. Hide it when the giver visits.

Afternoon in Madrid

BLAST OFF!

SCIENTISTS HAVE DISCOVERED that a powerful spray of water can destroy up to 90 percent of aphid and mite problems. So put your plants in the tub or sink, and spray until they're drenched.

HOUSEPLANT HOSPITAL

SICK PLANTS showing signs of distress should be isolated from your healthy population. First, move them to a well-lit recovery area with good air circula-tion. Then treat the soil and the plants with Seventh Generation's Heavy Duty Citrus Cleaner and Degreaser. For scale infestations, spot-treat with rubbing alcohol or Murphy's Oil Soap spray. And always pick up and dispose of diseased or fallen foliage.

The Canary in the Greenhouse

Beware if your ficus tree drops all its leaves for no visible reason; you may have a dangerous undetected gas leak in the house.

Forcing Garlic

Hyacinths aren't the only plants that thrive in a glass forcing-vase. To ensure a winter supply of fresh garlic leaves, place a whole head of organic garlic, which is not treated with a sprouting inhibitor, atop the narrowed mouth of a forcing-vase. Fill the vase with water until it barely touches the bottom of the garlic and set it in a sunny western or southern window.

ISOLATION WARD

WATCH YOUR PATIENT for two weeks, and if it continues to languish, trim diseased foliage, dose it again, water, and cover it with a large, clear plastic isolation bag taped tightly around the container.

In a week, check again for signs of recurring pests. Be sure to look on the under-sides of leaves and along stems. If all is well, move the plant back into the mainstream population. Sadly, when all else fails, it's sometimes necessary to dump a plant and begin anew with a healthy specimen.

VACATION TIME

IF YOU CAN'T find anyone dependable to care for your indoor plants while you're on vacation (up to two weeks), take these easy steps to ensure their well-being.

Groom, thoroughly soak, and feed your plants, then cluster them together in an empty

bathtub or child's swimming pool.
Set in a sunny location or provide
your plants with artificial lighting
while you're away. Cover them
completely with a lightweight
tent of clear plastic, and tightly
seal it with tape on all sides.
For a longer vacation (three
weeks), see the directions
(page 95) for making a capillary
mat to set below the plants in
a bathtub.

WICK-IT GOOD

SET YOUR WATERED and
fed houseplants on a sheet of
plastic or in the bathtub. Fill
a large bucket (at least 5 gallons) with water and set it on a stool
or chair, beside and higher than the plants. Cut ½-inch-thick cotton rope
into pieces long enough to reach from the bucket to each pot. Set one end of
the rope into the bottom of the bucket. Drape the remainder of the rope onto
the soil, and coil it around a plant. The wicking action of the cotton rope
will keep your plants watered while you're away.

You can run as many pieces of rope as necessary, but be aware that the
more wicks you use, the more quickly the water level drops. You may want to
lay a piece of plastic beneath the rope in case it drips.

SPRING FORWARD

GO OUTDOORS in late February and cut a long, graceful branch of spirea, forsythia, plum, cherry, apple, or willow. Make a 2-inch slit in the base of the stem with a sharp knife. Plunge the branch immediately into a tall vase of warm water. Watch closely during the next month as the branches burst into glorious bloom, then cloak themselves in vibrant (and welcome) green leaves. Be sure to change the water every week.

THE CAT'S MEOW

DISTRACT YOUR CATS from your favorite house-plants by sowing a tasty "lawn" of red wheat for them. Purchase wheat seeds, also known as wheat berries, at a health-food store. Prepare a shallow container (or several, depending on the number of cats) with fresh potting soil. Sprinkle a thick covering of seeds on top of the soil, and water it gently. Set the container in a warm, well-lit area out of the reach of your feline friend. Within a few days, the wheat will sprout. When it's a couple of inches tall, put it some-where accessible so your cats can snack on this health-food and leave your houseplants alone.

Forced early-spring apple blossoms.

TEMPORARY TRANSPLANT

NOT ALL YOUR relationships with houseplants need be long-term commitments. Some of the most ephemeral encounters can be the most pleasurable.

Browse your favorite nursery for the most seasonal and sensational plants available—say, 4-foot delphiniums or foxgloves. Purchase a few of them with the understanding that they'll be doing indoor duty, something they may not be accustomed to.

Line a basket with plastic, which you can disguise with a layer of moss, and fill the basket with a clutch of plants such as primroses, pansies, nemesias, snapdragons, bacopa (for a lacy border), poppies, and nasturtiums. Keep the plants in their original containers, or transplant them into small pots. Use this display for a windowsill or as a unique centerpiece for your table. (After ten days, transplant them outdoors.)

Wardian Case

This nearly airtight case was named for its inventor, Nathaniel Ward, who in 1836 miniaturized a traditional greenhouse and adapted it for transporting plants on long sea voyages. Wardian cases are the perfect environment for ferns, mosses, and any plants that flourish in high humidity. The best placement is out of direct sunlight (so as not to burn tender leaves).

Calendula

Appendix

Cosmos

PLANTS FOR BENEFICIAL INSECTS

NECTAR- AND POLLEN-RICH PLANTS

COMMON NAME	GENUS
Aster	*Aster* spp.
Bee balm	*Monarda didyma*
Black-eyed Susan	*Rudbeckia hirta*
Blueberry	*Vaccinium* spp.
Borage	*Borago officinalis*
Buckwheat	*Eriogonum* spp.
Butterfly bush	*Buddleia davidii*
Calendula	*Calendula officinalis*
Catmint	*Nepeta* spp.
Chives	*Allium schoenoprasum*
Coneflower	*Echinacea* spp.
Coral bell	*Heuchera* spp.
Cosmos	*Cosmos bipinnatus*

Borage

Tithonia

Jewelweed

COMMON NAME	GENUS
Dill	*Anethum graveolens*
Fennel	*Foeniculum vulgare*
Flowering currant	*Ribes sanguineum*
Flowering tobacco	*Nicotiana* spp.
Foxglove	*Digitalis* spp.
Goldenrod	*Solidago* spp.
Hollyhock	*Alcea rosea*
Jewelweed	*Impatiens capensis*
Joe-pye weed and boneset	*Eupatorium* spp.
Lantana	*Lantana* spp.
Lavender	*Lavandula* spp.
Lilac	*Syringa vulgaris*
Lupine	*Lupinus* spp.
Milkweed/Butterfly weed	*Asclepias* spp.
Phlox	*Phlox* spp.
Pincushion flower	*Scabiosa* spp.
Pineapple sage	*Salvia elegans*
Redbud	*Cercis canadensis*
Sedum	*Sedum spectabile*
Sunflower	*Helianthus* spp.
Verbena and vervain	*Verbena* spp.
Willow	*Salix* spp.
Zinnia	*Zinnia* spp.

LARVAL HOST PLANTS

COMMON NAME	GENUS
Aster	*Aster* spp.
Borage	*Borago officinalis*
Dill	*Anethum graveolens*
Fennel	*Foeniculum vulgare*
Hollyhock (singles)	*Alcea rosea*
Hop vine	*Humulus lupulus*
Lupine	*Lupinus* spp.
Marigold	*Tagetes* spp.
Milkweed	*Asclepias* spp.
Parsley	*Petroselinum crispum*
Pipevine	*Aristolochia* spp.
Plumbago	*Plumbago* spp.
Queen Anne's lace	*Daucus carota*
Violets	*Viola* spp.

Violets

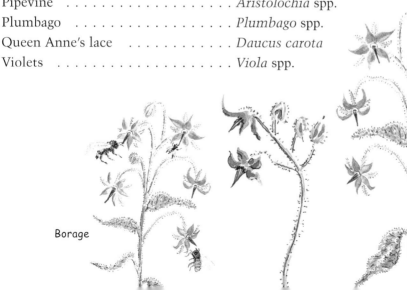

Borage

CRITTER HOUSING

NATIVE ORCHARD MASON BEE APARTMENTS

USE 4-INCH by 4-inch cedar posts (never use the chemically treated wood), and vary the heights from 3 feet to 5 feet.

Give your apartments the appearance of a hip roofed structure by cutting each side of the posts at a 60-degree angle to form a point.

Drill a row of $\frac{5}{16}$-inch holes, $\frac{3}{4}$ of an inch on center and 3 inches deep. I've used four columns across and six rows of holes, but there are no rules as to number.

Use tin, aluminum, or copper cut to fit the roof, and glue it in place to protect the wood and bees from moisture. Sink posts 1 foot deep into the soil or concrete, with the entry holes facing east.

Cedar post bee havens add a sculptural element to the landscape.

BUMBLEBEE ABODE

FIND A SHELTERED, shady area, and set a flat rock on the ground. Lay a handful of cotton or fine, dry

grasses on the rock. With a masonry bit, drill a ⅝-inch entry hole into the side of a 6-inch terra-cotta pot. This opening is large enough for bees, but too small for mice. Set the pot over the grasses and place a brick or flat stone on top of the pot to cover the drainage hole (bee nests must be kept dry) and to discourage marauding skunks.

BAT HOUSE

FOR INSTRUCTIONS in building or for a bat house kit, contact the Organization for Bat Conservation (OBC). (See page 192.)

POLLINATORS IN A CAN

GATHER DRY SUNFLOWER stalks, slender shoots of bamboo, or pithy berry canes and cut them into 6-inch lengths. Thoroughly clean and dry a large can (6-inch depth is best) and camouflage the exterior by painting it dull brown, green, or gray. Screw the back of the can to a piece of wood. Tightly stuff the can with the stalks or canes and mount it horizontally in a tree or other shady, protected location, such as against a fence or wall.

Mount bat houses at least 15 feet above the garden.

SALAMANDER "HIGH-RISE"

Materials you'll need:

LOGS 2½ INCHES TO 3 INCHES IN DIAMETER AND 15 INCHES LONG

GALVANIZED DECK SCREWS 3½ INCHES TO 4½ INCHES LONG (AT LEAST

1 INCH LONGER THAN THE WIDTH OF YOUR LOGS)

AN ELECTRIC SCREWDRIVER OR DRILL

PLACE FOUR LOGS parallel on the ground about 1 inch apart, and then four more logs perpendicular to and on top of the first row about 1 inch apart. Install the deck screws through the top logs to secure them to the log below. Lay another row of four logs perpendicular to and on top of the second row about 1 inch apart. Repeat the installation of deck screws and alternating rows of logs until you've reached the desired height. Site the log high-rise in a sheltered, shady area.

Drop leaves and organic yard debris (not treated with pesticides or herbicide) down between the logs. Keep poisons and slug and snail baits away from this area.

WORM COMPOST BINS

INDOOR WORM BIN

Materials you'll need:

> A LIDDED PLASTIC CONTAINER AT LEAST 2 FEET BY 3 FEET
> AND 18–20 INCHES DEEP
> SCREEN (TO LINE THE BOTTOM)
> A TRAY (TO CATCH THE MOISTURE)
> 4 BRICKS TO ELEVATE THE CONTAINER

POKE 1/4-INCH DRAINAGE HOLES in the bottom and air holes in the sides and the lid. Cover the floor of the container with screen and a layer of moist, shredded  newspaper. Add some kitchen leftovers and worms. *Always* top the worms with more wet newspaper, cardboard, or grass clippings after adding garbage. Fill one half of the container before moving to the other side. Empty the full half and repeat the process. Always keep the lid on the box.

BIN MENU: Spread a layer of bedding (shredded wet newspaper or cardboard, grass clippings, pine needles, leaves (nothing containing pesticides, herbicides, rodenticides, fungicides) before adding household garbage, including eggshells, coffee grounds (and filters), and tea bags.

Moisten your worm bin
once a week.

Worms

Flowerfield Enterprises

10332 Shaver Road

Kalamazoo, MI 49024-6744

www.wormwoman.com

nancy@wormwoman.com

(269) 327-0108

(269) 327-7009 fax

Vermicomposting

products

OUTDOOR CINDER BLOCK WORM BIN

YOU CAN BUILD a 4-foot by 8-foot worm bin 30 inches tall with a plywood top for approximately $100. The cinder blocks will last a lifetime, and your bin can be disassembled and moved if desired.

Materials you'll need:

> 64 CINDER BLOCKS 8 INCHES BY 8 INCHES BY 16 INCHES
>
> A 4-FOOT BY 8-FOOT SHEET OF ⅜-INCH EXTERIOR PLYWOOD
>
> A FLAT, SHADY SPOT AT LEAST 4 FEET BY 8 FEET

START WITH A ROW of cinder blocks to form the sides of a rectangle 4 feet by 8 feet. Lay the blocks end to end with the holes facing up. For the first row, use six blocks for the front and back sides. Use two blocks on each of the two ends and butting into the front and back.

For the second row, stagger the blocks to overlap the first row by using three blocks on each of the two ends and five along the front and back, butting into the sides. Repeat the first-row pattern for the third row, and the second-row pattern for the fourth. The height can be easily adjusted by using fewer or more rows of blocks.

Cut the plywood into two 4-foot by 4-foot pieces. Fit the plywood to cover the top of the bin. Don't situate the bin against a wooden fence or siding.

If you live in an extremely cold area, lay 2-inch-thick pieces of Styrofoam against the sides of the bin and cut two pieces to "float" on top of the garbage in the bin. Worms slow down in cold weather and may overwinter in the cocoon stage.

To keep the contents smelling fresh and looking acceptable, always cover garbage with a layer of bedding. Foods not recommended for worm consumption are cheese, butter, meat, and oily products.

LIGHTING THE INDOOR GARDEN

NORTHERN EXPOSURE

THESE RESILIENT PLANTS will thrive in the pale but constant light of a northern exposure: *Aspidistras, Muehlenbeckia* (the dainty but hardy maidenhair vine), an amazing array of ferns, asparagus smilax vine (one of the most popular bouquet and decorative plants of Victorian times), ivies, ficus, philodendrons, Chinese evergreens, marlberry, Norfolk Island pine (also a nice holiday decoration), variegated aucuba, palms, peperomia, mother-in-law's tongue, umbrella tree, and spathiphyllum.

SUNNY SOUTHERN DISPOSITIONS

IF YOU'RE DREAMING of an indoor jungle of flowers, your sunny southern window is the place to cultivate that desire. Experiment with elegant mandevilla vines, hibiscus, and cyclamen (both florist's and miniatures). Lemon verbena, one of the most potently scented of all herbs, will happily grow indoors. But beware—come winter it will shed its leaves. Try your hand with dwarf fruit trees (which need night temperatures of 55 degrees) such as the tasty Meyer's lemon, kumquats, limes, "Chinotto" orange, figs, and pomegranates. Abutilons, also known as flowering maples, with their drooping, hoop-skirted blossoms, will thrive and bloom prolifically alongside hibiscus, lantana (they need strong light three hours a day), climbing polyanthum jasmine (easy to train into a circular form), clerodendrums, geraniums, pentas, and scented pelargoniums.

Lemon
verbena

EASTERN INFLUENCE

THESE STALWART PLANTS will flourish in the evanescent morning light of an east-facing window: rex begonias, angel-wing begonias, forcing bulbs (narcissus, daffodils, hyacinths, muscari, crocus, anemones, lily-of-the-valley), fuchsias (try the miniature thymifolia—it forms perfect topiaries), citrus, hoyas, whimsical windmill jasmine, impatiens, streptocarpus, orchids, violets, gesneriads (always water from below and don't splash their hairy leaves with water), and clivia and amaryllis (two winter bloomers with brilliant flowers).

THE WILD WEST

NEAR A WESTERN window, nestle some fuchsias, coddle a pittosporum and revel in its flowers scented like orange blossoms, and reserve an area for a stately, shiny-leaved camellia studded with perfect rosette blooms. Hoyas, alocasias (with their architectural leaf shapes and veining), anthuriums (so many varieties from which to choose), and calatheas (the zebra-striped *Zebrina* is striking) also enjoy this setting.

Geranium

INCANDESCENT BULBS

MANY HOUSEPLANTS are content to grow and bloom beneath overhanging lamps outfitted with incandescent lightbulbs. Keep 40-watt bulbs at least 16 inches away from plants, 60-watt bulbs 24 inches away, and 100- to 150-watt bulbs about 30 inches above the plants.

GRO-LIGHTS

THESE SMALL BULBS are rated R-25, come in 50, 75, and 150 watts, and cost about $6 each. Use them for focused lighting on specimens such as ficus trees or over a collection of violets, pelargoniums, streptocarpus, or herbs.

HIGH-INTENSITY DISCHARGE (HID)

NEW HID LIGHTS have two to three times the output of fluorescent light tubes. A typical 400-watt HID, which uses 6 kilowatts per hour, will furnish enough lumens for a grouping of light-loving bloomers (see the plants listed under Sunny Southern Dispositions, opposite page).

FLUORESCENT BULBS AND TUBES

CLUSTER YOUR PLANTS below fluorescent bulbs, or string them along the length of a fluorescent tube. Try blending fluorescents by using both a cool white and a warm white tube. Hang the fixture about 20 inches above your plants. The strongest light is in the center, so group your scented pelargoniums, violets, and orchids there, and place the plants with low-light requirements (see Shady Characters, page 153) at both ends of the tube.

Fare Thee Well

Resources

Garden and Insect Suppliers

COAST OF MAINE ORGANIC PRODUCTS, INC.
145 Newbury Street
Portland, ME 04101
www.coastofmaine.com
sales@coastofmaine.com
(800) 345-9315
(207) 879-0554 fax
Fermented salmon fertilizer

DR. BRONNER'S MAGIC SOAP
P.O. Box 28
Escondido, CA 92033
www.drbronner.com
allone@drbronner.com
(760) 743-2211
(760) 745-6675 fax

ENTOMOS, LLC
4445 SW 35th Terrace, Suite 310
Gainesville, FL 32608
www.entomos.com
info@entomos.com
(866) 371-6490 toll-free
(352) 371-6490
(352) 371-4181 fax
Beneficial insects

GARDENS ALIVE!
5100 Schenley Place
Lawrenceburg, IN 47025
www.gardensalive.com
gardenhelp@gardensalive.com
(812) 537-8651 information
(812) 537-8650 sales
(812) 537-5108 fax orders
Beneficial insects and garden supplies,
Surround At Home (kaolin spray)

PEACEFUL VALLEY FARM SUPPLY
P.O. Box 2209
Grass Valley, CA 95945
www.groworganic.com
contact@groworganic.com
(888) 784-1722 orders
(530) 272-4769
(530) 272-4794 fax
Supplier of insects, beneficial insect
lures, tools, organic fertilizer

PLANTEA, INC.
P.O. Box 1980
Kodiak, AK 99615
www.plantea.com
marion@plantea.com
(800) 253-6331
(907) 486-2500
(907) 486-2686 fax
PlanTea, the organic plant food packed
in convenient tea bags; unique gardening
tools; tips; unusual recipes

RINCON-VITOVA INSECTARIES, INC.
P.O. Box 1555
Ventura, CA 93002
www.rinconvitova.com
bugnet@rinconvitova.com
(800) 248-2847 (BUGS)
(805) 643-5407
(805) 643-6267 fax
Beneficial insects

Heirloom Roses

ANTIQUE ROSE EMPORIUM
9300 Lueckemeyer Rd.
Brenham, TX 77833
www.weareroses.com
(800) 441-0002
(979) 836-9051 (Customer Service)
(979) 836-0928 fax

HEIRLOOM OLD GARDEN ROSES
24062 N.E. Riverside Dr.
St. Paul, OR 97137
www.heirloomroses.com
info@heirloomroses.com
(503) 538-1576
(503) 538-5902 fax
Catalog $5

Heirloom Seed Suppliers

AMISHLAND HEIRLOOM SEEDS
P.O. Box 365
Reamstown, PA 17567
amishlandseeds@netscape.net
(717) 738-0134

JOHNNY'S SELECTED SEEDS
184 Foss Hill Road
Albion, ME 04910
www.johnnyseeds.com
info@johnnyseeds.com
(207) 437-9294
(800) 738-6314 fax
(207) 437-2675 fax outside
continental U.S.
Heirloom and organic seeds

LANDIS VALLEY MUSEUM
Heirloom Seed Project
2451 Kissel Hill Road
Lancaster, PA 17601
www.landisvalleymuseum.org/
seeds.htm
(717) 569-0401
(717) 560-2147 fax

NATIVE SEEDS/SEARCH
526 N. 4th Avenue
Tucson, AZ 85705
www.nativeseeds.org
info@nativeseeds.org

(520) 622-5561
(520) 622-5591 fax

SEED SAVERS EXCHANGE
3076 North Winn Road
Decorah, IA 52101
www.seedsavers.org
catalog@seedsavers.org
(563) 382-5990
(563) 382-5872 fax
Seed Savers: free 80-page color seed
catalog

For additional seed companies, see
Roots, Shoots, Buckets & Boots (New
York: Workman Publishing, 1999), or
visit www.sharonlovejoy.com/cat.html

Organizations

**AMERICAN HORTICULTURAL
SOCIETY**
7931 East Boulevard Drive
Alexandria, VA 22308
www.ahs.org
(800) 777-7931
(703) 768-5700
(703) 768-8700 fax

**BAT CONSERVATION
INTERNATIONAL**
P.O. Box 162603
Austin, TX 78716
www.batcon.org/batinfo@batcon.org
(800) 538-BATS (2287) orders
(512) 327-9721
(512) 327-9724 fax

**BIO-INTEGRAL RESOURCE CENTER
(BIRC)**
P.O. Box 7414
Berkeley, CA 94707
www.birc.org
birc@igc.org
(510) 524-2567
(510) 524-1758 fax

CORNELL LAB OF ORNITHOLOGY
159 Sapsucker Woods Rd.
Ithaca, NY 14850
www.birds.cornell.edu
cornellbirds@cornell.edu
(800) 843-BIRD (2473)
(607) 254-2473

NATIONAL AUDUBON SOCIETY
700 Broadway
New York, NY 10003
www.audubon.org
(212) 979-3000
(212) 979-3188 fax

NATIONAL WILDLIFE FEDERATION
National Wildlife Federation Backyard
Habitat Program
11100 Wildlife Center Drive
Reston, VA 20190-5362
www.nwf.org
www.nwf.org/backyardwildlifehabitat
info@nwf.org
(800) 822-9919
(703) 438-6000
(703) 438-6294 Backyard Habitat Program
(703) 438-6468 fax

**ORGANIZATION FOR BAT
CONSERVATION (OBC) AT
CRANBROOK INSTITUTE OF
SCIENCE**
39221 Woodward Avenue
Bloomfield Hills, MI 48303
www.batconservation.org
obcbats@aol.com
(800) 276-7074
(248) 645-3242 fax

XERCES SOCIETY
4828 S.E. Hawthorne Boulevard
Portland, OR 97215-3252
www.xerces.org
info@xerces.org
(503) 232-6639
(503) 233-6794 fax

An international nonprofit organization
focused on invertebrates and
conservation projects

Further Reading

Brenzel, Kathleen Norris, ed. *Sunset Western Garden Book.* Menlo Park, CA: Sunset Publishing Corp., 2001.

Brickell, Christopher, ed. *The American Horticultural Society Encyclopedia of Garden Plants.* New York: Macmillan Publishing Co., 1989.

Buchmann, Stephen L., and Gary Paul Nabham. *The Forgotten Pollinators.* Washington, D.C.: Island Press, 1996.

Duke, James A., Ph.D. *The Green Pharmacy.* Emmaus, Penn.: Rodale Press, 1997.

Engel, Cindy. *Wild Health.* New York: Houghton Mifflin Co., 2002.

Hadidian, John , Guy R. Hodge, and John W. Grandy, eds. *Wild Neighbors: The Humane Approach to Living with Wildlife*. Golden, Colorado: Fulcrum Publishing, 1997.

Hickman, Mae, and Maxine Guy. *Care of the Wild Feathered and Furred*. New York: Michael Kesund Publishing, 1998.

Miller, Crow. *Let's Get Growing: A Dirt-Under-the-Nails Primer on Raising Vegetables, Fruits and Flowers Organically*. Emmaus, Penn.: Rodale Press, 1995.

Olkowski, William , Sheila Daar, and Helga Olkowski. *The Gardener's Guide to Common-Sense Pest Control*. Newton, Conn.: Tauton Press, 1995.

Pollan, Michael. *Second Nature*. Boston: Atlantic Monthly Press, 1991.

Pyle, Robert Michael. *Field Guide to North American Butterflies*. New York: Alfred A. Knopf, 1981.

Sandbeck, Ellen. *Slug Bread & Beheaded Thistles*. New York: Broadway Books, 2000.

Sibley, David Allen. *The Sibley Guide to Birds*. New York: Alfred A. Knopf, 2001.

Tekulsky, Mathew. *The Butterfly Garden: Turning Your Garden, Window Box or Backyard into a Beautiful Home for Butterflies*. Boston: The Harvard Common Press, 1985.

Tuttle, Merlin D. *America's Neighborhood Bats*. Austin, Texas: University of Texas Press, 1988.

Williams, Kim, and Rob Mies. *Understanding Bats*. Marietta, Ohio: Bird Watcher's Digest Press, 1996.

Xerces Society, in association with the Smithsonian Institution. *Butterfly Gardening: Creating Summer Magic in Your Garden*. San Francisco: Sierra Club Books, 1990.

Index